THE
MANUAL OF
ILLUSTRATION
TECHNIQUES

The
Manual of
Illustration
Techniques

A & C Black • London

A QUARTO BOOK

Published in the United Kingdom in 2003
by A&C Black Publishers Limited
37 Soho Square
London W1D 3QZ

ISBN 0-7136-6650-1

QUAR.EIT

This book was designed and produced by
Quarto Publishing
The Old Brewery
6 Blundell Street
London N7 9BH

Senior editor: Kate Kirby
Senior art editor: Elizabeth Healey
Designer: James Hitchens
Editors: Patricia Seligman, Hazel Harrison
Photographers: Martin Norris, Chas Wilder, Jon Wyand
Picture manager: Giulia Hetherington
Editorial editor: Mark Dartford
Art directors: Moira Clinch, Penny Cobb

Typeset by Central Southern Typesetters, Eastbourne
Manufactured in Hong Kong by Regent Pub. Services Ltd
Printed in China by Leefung-Asco Printers Ltd

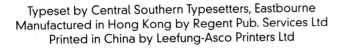

CONTENTS

INTRODUCTION

How many times have you said to yourself, "I wish I could do that!" and in the next breath given reasons for the impossibility of achieving your desire. "I wish I could draw like that, but I don't have the talent," is a statement commonly heard, and I remember saying much the same thing to myself as I looked through all my favorite illustrated books and longed to create such pictures. But with determination and a little advice, it is possible for anyone to create wonderful and exciting images. This book provides the latter, so all you need is the determination, the vital ingredient of talent.

When I first left college I started with a rudimentary portfolio, a couple of sketchbooks, lots of enthusiasm, but little else, and consequently was completely unprepared for a career as a freelance illustrator. Thankfully, colleges these days have become more experienced at offering their students guidance and information on how to set up in this profession, but finding that first job that will lead to others is still a daunting challenge for the graduate. The problem is even greater for the amateur illustrator, who has not gained the confidence instilled by a college course. I found that many of the books available seemed to specialize in techniques more suitable for the fine artist, while those that were written for the illustrator concentrated on style and medium, giving little or no advice on how to turn illustration into a successful career. Now that I lecture in illustration myself, I am even more acutely aware of the need for good literature to help students and amateurs and enable them to obtain good professional advice. Thus when planning this book I felt it was essential to show only the work of successful freelance illustrators, both in the "themes" section, which contains a wide selection of finished illustrations, and in the technique step-by-step demonstrations. I have not neglected practical advice, and the book includes a section on going professional. Here you will see some professional illustrators' portfolios, which hopefully will inspire you to design one of your own.

Illustration is not an easy career to chose, not least because it often demands long working days to meet short deadlines, and can lead to quite an isolated life. However, there is nothing more exciting than landing your first job and then seeing it appear in print. I look forward to seeing yours.

TECHNIQUES

How an illustrator manipulates a medium can be as unique as a fingerprint. Each artist creates his or her own technique using one or a variety of mediums; ultimately this becomes an individual style. Technique is the starting point, but makes up only a part of the illustration; the rest is a combination of strong drawing skills, understanding color, and composition and design ability.

The following section looks at the wide variety of techniques, both traditional and modern, available to the professional and amateur illustrator, from the time-honored techniques of watercolor, to new and exciting innovations in computer technology.

This section includes detailed descriptions of each technique and includes information on the materials, tools and equipment required. Particular attention is focused on the media and techniques that assist the busy illustrator, where alternatives to traditional media can help speed up the creative process. Techniques are demonstrated with step-by-step sequences by professional illustrators who specialize in that particular medium or technique.

It is important to remember that these demonstrations are only basic guidelines, helping you to acquire practical knowledge of each technique and medium. It is your own exploration and experimentation that will help you to create your own unique style.

ACRYLICS
This medium can be used in a whole variety of ways including mimicking other mediums (see p.10). In this illustration it has been used to imitate watercolor, by using the pigment with water to create a series of glazes.

LINE AND WASH
This technique (see p.62) helps you to create solid strong forms extremely quickly; as the black ink outline develops the shape and detail, the color is added with flat watercolor washes.

COLORED PENCILS
Traditionally colored pencil is used either for sketching, or to create soft images (see p.34). Here the illustrator has used a rough textured paper and the pencil in layers to create intense saturated color, not usually associated with this medium.

Acrylic

THE WONDER OF ACRYLIC PAINTS IS THEIR ENORMOUS VERSATILITY, WHICH MAKES THEM AN OBVIOUS CHOICE FOR THE ILLUSTRATOR. THEY CAN BE SPRAYED, SCRAPED, SQUEEZED, GIVEN TEXTURE, AND EVEN WOVEN.

Acrylics are water-based paints which can be used to imitate effects produced by traditional oils and watercolors. Both opaque techniques working from dark to light, and transparent ones, working from light to dark, are possible.

BASIC EQUIPMENT Either synthetic or natural-hair brushes are suitable for use with acrylics. Hair brushes are more expensive, but they last longer as they don't clog up as quickly. Acrylics can be used on virtually any surface—paper, cardboard, board, plastic, or metal. There is a wide range of complementary substances that can be mixed with acrylic paint to produce different effects: **gloss medium** increases color transparency, producing a glossy finish useful for glazing techniques; **matt medium** also increases

Paola Piglia
Here acrylic paint has been used in successive layers, with the paint applied sparingly using a dry-brush technique.

the transparency but retains the natural, non-reflective nature of the medium; **gel medium** thickens the paint but keeps the transparency; **flow improver** is used instead of water to prevent loss of color strength; **retarder** is used to delay drying; and various **modeling pastes** can be used to give body to the paint for greater textural effects.

APPLICATIONS FOR THE ILLUSTRATOR As a medium for illustration, acrylic is becoming increasingly popular, because it allows a wide range of techniques and is easy to handle. This means the illustrator can develop his or her own unique style. Acrylic also reproduces well because of the solidity and clarity of its colors. Works in acrylic can be found in all areas of illustration from books to advertising and cartoon work.

GETTING STARTED As the uses of acrylic are so diverse, it takes time to develop a high level of skill in this medium. It is a medium, though, that is kind to the beginner, inviting experimentation.

The most common form of acrylic is a plastic latex or emulsion, soluble in water. It can be applied in a thin wash or in transparent glazes as in watercolor. It is also possible to apply these paints thickly in a rich impasto style as in oil painting. For the illustrator, acrylics are simpler and more useful than oil paints as they dry quickly, allowing colors to be overlaid more rapidly. They are also sturdier and more flexible, adhering to almost any surface.

MARK MAKING
The ground—the paper or other surface—is important in acrylic painting, as it is for most drawing and painting media. Depending on this and on the technique used, a wide variety of effects can be created.
❶ Hot-pressed paper with a wet acrylic wash.
❷ Not paper with a drier wash.
❸ Rough paper with a dragged dry wash.

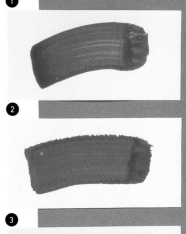

☞
Airbrushing; Collage and Mixed Media; Corrections; Enlarging and Scaling up; Line and Wash; Linework.

MIXING ACRYLIC PAINT

Acrylic paint can be mixed with a wide variety of media, allowing the illustrator to produce numerous effects.

1 | A clean white palette allows you to see your color mixes as they will appear on white paper. Brushes can be washed out in clean water.

2 | An old plate or a metal sheet or tray make excellent palettes too. The paint can be either washed off with water or allowed to dry and then scraped off. Some artists just let the paint build up and mix over the top.

TRANSPARENT ACRYLIC

Acrylic paint can be applied in a very similar way to watercolor, that is in layers of transparent washes. But it behaves differently, drying quickly to an impermeable surface, with no chances to soften an edge with water or blend in more color. This can be an advantage, too, allowing you to build up crisp layers, wet-on-dry, which will not blend together.

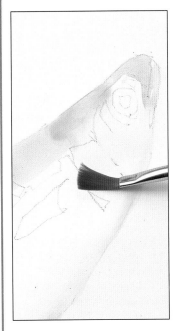

1 | To create the same effect as watercolor washes, acrylic paint can be mixed either with water, gel coat, or a solution of water-tension breaker. It is then applied in much the same way as watercolor, using similar grounds and brushes. Start with the palest washes.

2 | Each wash is applied and then allowed to dry, gradually building up the color with layers of darker pigment. As on the body of the fish, it is also possible to work wet-in-wet, dropping more color into a previously applied wash quickly before it dries.

3 | Highlights and reflections are applied at the end, with undiluted white acrylic paint.

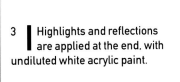

4 | This technique allows you to create a wide variety of colors and tones by applying them as washes one over the other, much like laying sheets of colored glass over each other.

OPAQUE ACRYLIC

Acrylic paint can be used in a very similar way to oil paint, allowing you to paint light over dark. But the two media behave very differently. Acrylic paint dries much more quickly than oil paint, which leaves you little time to work the paints. The paint also dries darker, making it difficult to match colors. But for wet-on-dry techniques, the faster-drying acrylics are a great advantage. Generally, for the illustrator with pressing deadlines, acrylic has the advantage.

1 | Acrylic paint is applied first as an overall background using a chisel brush. The pigment covers the whole area, leaving no white paper showing, but the surface is uneven.

2 | Once the paint has dried, the next layer can be added. If the paint is drying too quickly, an acrylic "retarder" can be mixed into the pigment, which has the effect of slowing down the drying time.

3 | Once the bowl is dry, the orange fish and weed can be added over the top. A warm blue has been superimposed over part of the background to give a sense of depth.

4 | The final illustration is simple but effective. For the soft edges of the bowl, use a clean brush where the two colors meet to spread out the white paint.

TRANSPARENT OVER OPAQUE

Unlike watercolor and gouache, washes of acrylic paint can be laid successfully over each other without any danger of the first wash blending into the second. This allows the illustrator to apply numerous washes of glazes on top of one another.

1 | The acrylic paint is applied to the ground, (in this case a heavy watercolor paper). The paint is laid on quite thickly to give an opaque base.

2 | Once the base color has dried thoroughly, the transparent washes can be applied. A small amount of acrylic paint is mixed thoroughly into acrylic gel medium. This gives the paint an almost glass-like effect.

3 | The more gel medium added to the paint, the more transparent it becomes. This is a very useful technique for painting water, mist, reflections, and so on.

IMPASTO

When rendering texture such as foliage and fur, acrylic is ideal, as it is possible to apply it very thickly and thus hint at the texture of the subject standing out in relief from the surface of the paper. It is applied in much the same way as oil paint, but has the advantage that it dries much faster.

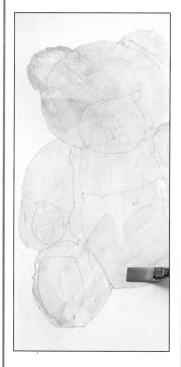

1 The outline of the design is first sketched out on the paper or watercolor board. Using a watered-down wash of acrylic paint, the paler mid-tone brown of the teddy is applied over the whole area.

2 The layers of color are then built up starting with the lighter shades, allowing each to dry before applying the next. As the darker colors are added, mix the paint to a thicker consistency each time.

3 Look carefully at your subject and observe the direction of the fur, etc. Then mirror the direction with strong, confident strokes of the brush.

4 It is very important to allow each layer of color to dry before applying the next. This process can be speeded up using a hairdryer.

5 To give your subject greater realism, use as wide a variety of tones as possible, the shadows almost black, the highlights. white. Add the areas of highlight in small thick impasto strokes to imitate the texture of the fur.

IMPASTO EFFECTS: BLENDING FIBERS

A variety of acrylic media to be mixed with acrylic paints to produce special effects are available. Here a medium containing blended fibers creates a rich impasto background. It can also be added to paints for areas of heavy texture.

IMPASTO EFFECTS: GLASS BEADS

Another medium produced especially to be mixed with acrylic paint is called Glass Beads, giving the effect of small beads of impasto.

1 | For a heavily textured ground, coat your support with a medium containing "blended fibers." You can apply it straight out of the pot, spooning it out and then leveling it with a flat brush.

3 | Allow the color to dry before applying further coats. Remember that the textured background will make it difficult to paint detail, so choose a simple design.

2 | Once the ground has dried (this process can be speeded up using a hairdryer), acrylic color can be applied all over the impasto surface.

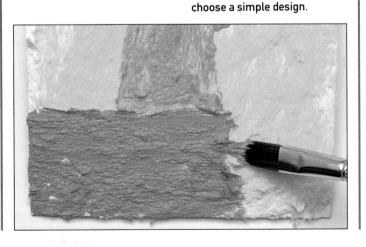

1 | In this example, to set off the texture to its best advantage, a flat, opaque wash of acrylic was applied to the ground and allowed to dry.

2 The textured gel is mixed with the acrylic paint using a clean brush and palette. The more gel added, the more textured the paint will become.

3 The texture is a little difficult to apply evenly, so it is not suitable to use for fine detailed work. Try to use broad designs and confident brushstrokes. Once dry, further layers of color can be applied over the top.

CRACKLE GLAZE

If you superimpose crackle glaze over an acrylic painting, you can recreate the surface craquelure which is found on old masters. The glaze is made up of two different solutions which must be applied in the correct order for the effect to work. It has a milky appearance at first, but after a few minutes it dries clear. Color can be added over the glaze to emphasize the cracks. It is also possible to add pigment to the top gel coat, which would give an even stronger impression of age.

1 The elephant has been painted onto board and allowed to dry thoroughly. The first gel solution is then applied, following instructions. To achieve a strong crackle, it should be applied quite thickly. It will not dry totally but will always feel sticky.

2 The second thinner coat can then be painted over the top. This coat will dry thoroughly and will also cause the coat underneath to dry.

3 Because the drying times are different, cracks appear in the top layer. To enhance the crackle effect, a darker or lighter shade of paint can be rubbed into the cracks, making them more distinct.

Airbrushing

AN AIRBRUSH CAN PRODUCE
ILLUSTRATIONS IN A PHOTO-REALISTIC
STYLE, WHICH CAN BE SO EFFECTIVE THAT
THEY ARE OFTEN MISTAKEN FOR THE REAL THING.

An airbrush is a paint gun that employs compressed air to atomize paint into a fine spray. It can be used to produce extremely fine detail or to fill in large areas of flat color. Photo-realistic pieces are built up with layers of carefully applied paint using various masking devices to protect certain areas from sprayed paint.

BASIC EQUIPMENT There are a variety of airbrushes on the market, each suitable for a different use. For large areas of flat color or graded tone, standard spray guns are most suitable. The more delicate the work, the more expensive the airbrush. Airbrushes use gravity or suction to feed paint to the nozzle. Airbrushes are usually powered by an air compressor, although it is possible, if expensive, to use aerosol cans of compressed air as a substitute. The compressor produces a constant and adjustable flow of air, to maintain an even spray of paint.

It is essential to wear a mask or respirator to avoid breathing in the small atomized droplets of paint which accumulate in the atmosphere. As the art of masking off areas of the support is part of the airbrusher's skill, useful pieces of equipment are masking film, latex masking fluid, and self-adhesive plastic film for masking on canvas. Masking tape of various widths is invaluable for creating sharp, straight edges and lines. You will also need a craft knife or scalpel.

The airbrush can be used with watercolor, acrylics, inks or oil paints, as long as the paint is free from lumps or particles that could block the nozzle.

APPLICATIONS FOR THE ILLUSTRATOR In recent years airbrushed artwork has lost popularity in favor of more expressive media. However, it can still be a very useful medium to have in an illustrator's repertoire. Illustrations for the car and motorbike industry have traditionally been airbrushed and it is particularly good for filling in backgrounds and applying glazes and shadows to brush artwork.

GETTING STARTED Although the original outlay on the airbrush is expensive, you can obtain excellent results in a relatively short period of time, and so save time and money in the long run. A high level of expertise is required for photo-realistic artwork, but the airbrush can be a useful and time-saving piece of equipment.

Before using an airbrush, practice using the trigger to vary the pressure which controls the flow of paint. This will allow you to use it as a brush or as a drawing tool.

When applying an overall flat tone with an opaque paint, it is important to move the brush evenly in overlapping parallel lines approximately 6–10 in. (15–25 cm) away from the surface. Thinner paints such as watercolor need to be held further away, approximately 20–24 in. (45–60 cm). With translucent paints it is also important to allow each "wash" to dry before applying the next. This prevents drips and unwanted mixing effects.

Masking, an art in itself, is a method of obtaining sharp straight edges and protecting certain areas from sprayed color. Stencils can be made of paper or of masking film that can be cut to shape before application.

Peter Bartczak
A whole range of airbrush techniques have been used in this image, from masking to spattering.

☞
Acrylic; Collage and Mixed Media; Corrections; Gouache; Markers; Masking Techniques; Watercolor.

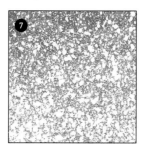

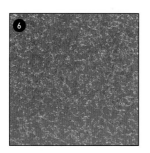

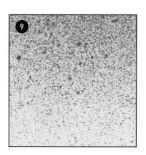

❶ *Flat color*
A standard nozzle was used for this effect at normal air pressure.
❷ *Overspraying using a standard nozzle*
Opaque paint used at full pressure, and repeated three times.
❸ *Overlapping transparent colors*
Three applications of 50% blue were applied over three applications of 50% red.

❹ *Graduated color*
Standard nozzle at 50% pressure creates a grainy effect.
❺ *Graduated color-mixing with transparent ink*
Color applied from 100% to 0% density using a standard nozzle, full pressure.
❻ *Graduated mixing with opaque gouache*
Gouache applied from 100% to 0% density, full pressure with splattercap nozzle, 1–3 applications.

❼ *Overspraying using a splattercap*
Opaque white is applied over a splattercap base, with 1–3 applications at full pressure.
❽ *Opaque color splatter*
Graduated splatter oversprayed at full pressure, 1–3 applications over opaque base.
❾ *Transparent color splatter*
Graduated color applied full pressure with splatter nozzle over transparent base color.

SPRAYING DISTANCES
Airbrush is similar to any drawing or painting medium in that it is possible to create a whole variety in the qualities of marks. With traditional media the mark is altered by varying the intensity of the pressure on the paper. With an airbrush the same effects can be obtained by varying the distance between the nozzle and the paper.

1 If the airbrush is held with the nozzle almost touching the surface, it will create a dense wide "brushmark." It is possible to guide the brush at the same distance, by resting your hand on the paper.

2 If you raise your hand and support your wrist on the paper, the line of paint becomes more diffuse.

The airbrush is a superb tool for creating fine, ultra-realistic detail.

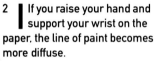

3 Raising your hand further, with your arm supported by the elbow, will create a broader even more diffuse line with a soft edge, the intensity of the pigment being diminished even further.

4 As with other drawing and painting media, a variety of line qualities will help you achieve different effects. This variety is particularly useful in freehand airbrush illustration.

PREPARATION

As airbrushing has many separate processes, before you start, make sure you have all the correct equipment and the appropriately prepared working area. In this example the illustrator has used a Hot Press paper, and is spraying watercolor over a watercolor underpainting.

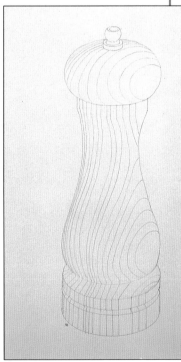

The design is first drawn very finely in pencil. If the lines are too dark they may show through the delicate watercolor washes. If your drawing is too heavy, it can be lightened by dabbing at the lines with a kneaded eraser.

UNDERPAINTING

An underpainting is not always necessary when airbrushing but it can enhance the final illustration. In this case it is used to add the fine detail of wood graining on the pepper grinder.

1 ▌A single pale wash is first applied all over the object, using a small sable brush. As this is a very tight technique, make sure the wash stays inside the outline.

2 ▌Once the first wash is dry, the detail of the graining can be added using a variety of darker washes. To achieve a realistic effect, apply the darker wash along the pencil line and then blend it outward.

MASKING

There are a number of masking techniques. In this example, two main methods are used. To protect the larger area of paper, a plain paper mask is made, which can be cut from cheaper layout or cartridge paper. This is not safe enough to use around the image itself, so for this area frisk, or masking, film is used, which is adhesive and therefore makes a reliable mask.

1 ▌Masking film is a semi-translucent plastic sheet which has one lightly adhesive surface. It comes in packs, each separate sheet attached to a backing paper which is removed before use. First, lay the film over the pepper grinder and the surrounding area. Rub it down, using a tissue, making sure that it overlaps the paper mask.

2 ▌Using a new scalpel blade, cut the film, following the edge of the object as accurately as possible. It is important to use the correct pressure necessary to cut the film without cutting the paper underneath, but it is not as difficult as it sounds.

3 ▌When the cut is complete, the excess film is then peeled back from the painting area. The film should come off very easily without removing any of the underlying washes.

OVERSPRAYING

In this example watercolor is used, although virtually any kind of paint can be used for this method, as long as it is thin enough to be sprayed through an airbrush nozzle.

1 | Using a sable brush, a watercolor wash of the right tone is loaded into the airbrush. Remember to clean out the airbrush between each wash, otherwise you end up with muddied colors.

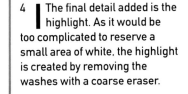

4 | The final detail added is the highlight. As it would be too complicated to reserve a small area of white, the highlight is created by removing the washes with a coarse eraser.

2 | Holding the brush approximately 4–6 in. (10–15 cm) away from the paper, the paint is applied in short bursts, with longer sprays to build up more color. Keep the brush moving while spraying.

3 | When sufficient paint has been applied to build up the desired tones, the frisk film can be removed. As shown in this example, the edges of the pepper mill are clean and sharp.

5 | The same masking process is followed for the shadow cast by the pepper mill. If you look carefully, it is possible to see that the shadow is darker nearer the pepper mill. This is achieved by applying more paint at the base of the object.

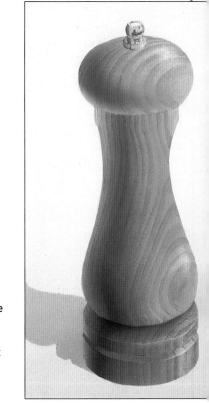

FREESTYLE AIRBRUSHING

Some airbrush illustrations are extremely involved and time-consuming, with many successive masks and sprayings. However, it is possible to create an image relatively quickly by using the airbrush in a freer, less controlled manner, without the use of masking film.

1 The image is first drawn out in pencil onto the paper (smoother papers are most suitable). The airbrush is then used to apply color, holding it close to the paper for a clean line. Mask the straight edge with a ruler.

2 To fill in larger areas and to lighten the tone, the airbrush is then held back from the paper. If you are a little unsure, use short bursts of the brush and build your confidence gradually, as you build up the darker tones.

3 Highlights are added as the final detail. Be very careful to clean out the brush thoroughly so the white paint is not tinted by any left-over pigment.

4 As can be seen in the finished illustration, the difference between freestyle and more traditional airbrushing techniques is that the latter has a clarity of line and an overall pristine appearance, while the freestyle method produces a softer, slightly fuzzy image.

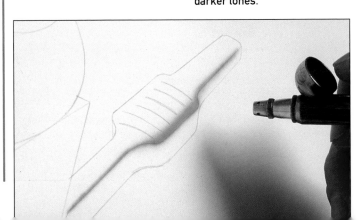

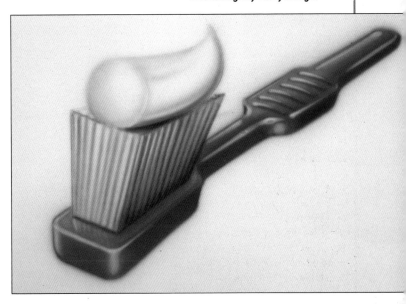

Brush drawing

BRUSHWORK IS AS PERSONAL AS HANDWRITING AND CAN BE USED AS A DISTINCTIVE STYLE OF ILLUSTRATION IN ITS OWN RIGHT TO CREATE IMAGES OF GREAT IMMEDIACY.

Brush drawing has been used throughout the centuries as a sensitive and expressive drawing technique, principally in China and Japan. Oriental artists were particularly interested in the nature of line itself. They found the brush to be a most effective tool, enabling them to render tone quickly and effectively as well as producing a symphony of different marks and flowing lines.

BASIC EQUIPMENT There is a close relationship in brush drawing between brush, ink, and paper, each affecting the line produced. There is a huge variety of brushes on the market, made of different hairs or synthetic fibers, and of different shapes and sizes, as well as traditional Chinese bamboo brushes. All are useful, since each creates its own particular mark. There is an even larger variety of papers to choose from, ranging from extremely fine, absorbent Chinese and Japanese papers to heavier western rag papers.

Traditionally, oriental stick or India ink have been used as the painting medium, but watercolor, acrylic or even oil paints can be very effective. But perhaps the most romantic are the oriental stick inks, scented with rosewater or musk, which are ground with water on an ink stone.

APPLICATIONS FOR THE ILLUSTRATOR As an illustration style, brush drawing is very effective. It is a speedy technique, which is always useful when having to meet short deadlines. Recently there has been a trend toward a more minimal, simpler approach in illustration, which is clearly achievable using this loose technique.

GETTING STARTED The secret of mastering this technique is to be relaxed and confident. Once this is achieved, you will find it an extremely good medium for self-expression.

It is best to begin with a large brush. Small ones encourage over-detailed work and can be inhibiting. Practice holding the brush in different positions and varying the pressures. This will help you to create a whole catalog of marks and lines. You will also learn how much ink or paint each of your brushes will hold. Try increasing and decreasing the amount of ink in the brush and using papers of different textures.

☞
Acrylic; Corrections;
Gouache; Line and Wash;
Linework; Markers;
Watercolor.

Michel Canetti
The success of the technique relies on the ability to describe an image through fluid expressive lines, an illustration gives the impression of having been formed completely effortlessly.

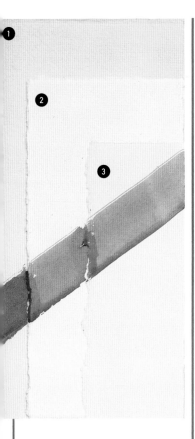

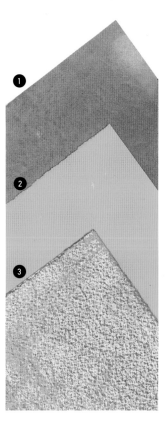

MIXING STICK INK

Any painting medium can be used for brush drawing, but it is great fun to experiment with traditional stick ink ground on an inkstone.

PAPER TEXTURES

Watercolor paper is probably the most popular support for brush drawing. It offers three different textures that will enhance an image in different ways.
❶ Hot-pressed paper has a fine, smooth surface.
❷ Not paper has a medium texture.
❸ Rough paper has a much heavier, more obvious, texture.

BRUSHMARKS

Brushes come in several different shapes and textures, and many different sizes. Each makes its own distinctive mark, so it is possible to achieve as many variations in brushmark as there are varieties of brush.
❶ Chinese bamboo brush.
❷ Ox-hair chisel brush.
❸ Acrylic one-stroke brush.
❹ Chisel bristle brush.

COLOR STRENGTH

The intensity or non-intensity of color relies on a number of factors including:
❶ The number of layers of color applied.
❷ The amount of water and pigment in the brush.
❸ The amount of pigment loaded onto the brush.

Pour a little water into the inkstone and grind the ink stick in it until you have the right density of color and texture. Too thick and it will not flow; too thin and it will run.

HOLDING THE BRUSH

Most of us have the tendency to hold our brushes and pencils far too tightly, which can be very restricting. Added to this, holding the brush as we would a pen tends to encourage movement only in one direction.

1 | This position for holding the brush uses the table to support the wrist.

2 | This hand position is often used by sign writers and is useful when working on a surface that is vertical or horizontal. The wrist rests on a brush or mahlstick, a stick with a padded end to prevent damage to the painting surface.

3 | Here the wrist is raised by resting only the elbow on the table. Variations can also be achieved by moving the fingers up and down the shaft of the brush; the higher the grip, the more freely the brush moves.

4 | This position is very useful for large illustrations. The whole arm and body may be used to move the brush freely across the paper. Try varying the pressure and angle of the brush to achieve variations in the character of the line.

Charcoal

CHARCOAL IS FOUND IN CAVE PAINTINGS, AND IT CONTINUES TO BE A MOST EXPRESSIVE MEDIUM.

Many will have tried this medium as children, because it is so simple to use. It is fast and extremely responsive, encouraging a boldness of approach, where mistakes can be integrated into the image or just as easily erased.

BASIC EQUIPMENT Charcoal is made from twigs of vine or willow, charred at high temperatures, in air-tight containers. There are different types and forms of charcoal, i.e. thin, medium, and thick willow, scene painters' charcoal, pencils, compressed sticks, and vine charcoal.

Any good-quality paper is suitable for this medium. However, the rougher, softer papers give the most dramatic effects. If you intend to use an eraser on your work, the paper surface will have to be strong enough to withstand such treatment. For the illustrator, it is most important to "fix" the charcoal onto the paper, to prevent the image from smudging. The commonly used fixatives are dilute solutions of either mastic or shellac, which can be bought in spray cans or in bottles. The bottled form is applied using a mouth blower.

Other useful equipment includes paper stumps or torchons for blending, feathers or a hairdryer to remove excess charcoal, and a soft kneaded (putty) eraser.

APPLICATIONS FOR THE ILLUSTRATOR Charcoal is commonly used for making preliminary drawings, but it can also be an expressive medium for finished pieces as can be seen in the work of the French artist Henri Matisse.

GETTING STARTED Charcoal is an extremely easy technique to use, with wide applications from the simplest sketch to highly worked studies. It is essential to relax your hand, and you will find that the fragility of the fine willow sticks will force you to do this.

There are two basic approaches to develop with charcoal, line and tone. Variations in line can be achieved by holding the stick in different positions in relation to the paper and using varying pressure. Subtle effects can be created using the grain of the paper to help build tone. Blending can be done with your finger or a paper stump, which is as effective, but less messy. Highlights can be created at the end by removing areas with the kneaded (putty) eraser.

☞
Colored Pencils; Corrections; Enlarging and Scaling up; Linework; Masking Techniques; Tracing and Transferring.

Philip Emms
A variety of charcoal techniques have been used in this illustration. Spontaneous fine lines for the hair, soft shading with a finger on the face, and shading with the side of the stick for the darker tones.

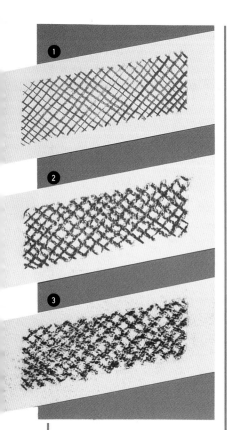

PAPER TEXTURES

As in any drawing or painting, the texture of the paper will affect the quality of the image. With charcoal, the more textured the paper the looser and grainier the line.

Charcoal hatching on:
1. Hot-pressed paper.
2. Not paper.
3. Rough paper.

MARK MAKING

Charcoal is not commonly used as an illustration medium for finished pieces as it is difficult to fix successfully. However, it is useful for trying out ideas and it can be mixed with other media, such as oil and chalk pastel. Used in this way, it can create strong atmospheric effects, so it is useful to experiment with different methods of application.

1 | To create a fine line with this medium, the stick is held at an angle to the paper. Vary the line and tone, altering the pressure on the stick.

2 | A broad stroke can be made by holding a short length of charcoal stick flat on the paper. Alter the width by breaking the stick to the size you need. The stick can also be pulled lengthwise or rotated as you go.

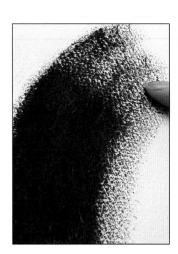

3 | Once the charcoal has been applied to the paper, it can be smudged with a finger. This softens the edge and creates a lighter tone.

To prevent constantly dirtying your fingers, a paper torchon can be used for shading.

USING A TORCHON

A torchon is made from rolled paper or sometimes even felt or leather. It is used for blending or smudging charcoal or pastels on paper to create graduated tones. It can also be used to apply the charcoal.

1 | A torchon can be used to move charcoal once it has been applied to the paper. A graduated tone is created by pulling the charcoal down in parallel strokes.

2 Charcoal can be applied to the end of a torchon to produce controlled soft areas of tone. This torchon is medium-sized; larger and smaller ones can also be obtained.

3 The torchon can be used with varying pressure to create different tones. This is a relatively slow process as the charcoal runs out quickly, so it is necessary to recharge the torchon regularly.

ADDING HIGHLIGHTS

With charcoal, highlights are simple to produce. As charcoal does not adhere very firmly to paper, you can easily remove small areas to reveal the white of the paper beneath.

Mold the end of a kneaded (putty) eraser into a point and remove an area of charcoal by rubbing in one direction. To save spoiling the next piece of work, make sure you cut the dirty bit off your eraser.

FIXING

It is essential to fix all charcoal work. An alternative to expensive canned fixative is hair spray. Always avoid inhaling fixative. Spray in a well-ventilated place.

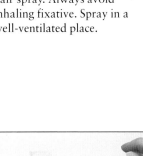

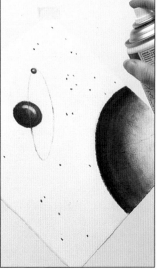

Hold the spray approximately 16 in. (45 cm) away from the paper and sweep the spray across and back evenly until the area is covered. This can be repeated once the first application dries.

FROTTAGE

Frottage can be created with a variety of media, oil and chalk pastel, wax crayon, as well as charcoal. Use it to create texture as part of an illustration, particularly in mixed media. Frottage textures are made with surfaces such as wood grain, textured metal, and even coarse fabric.

Lay the paper on the textured surface. With the flat of the charcoal stick, rub the paper firmly until the pattern is visible.

Collage and mixed media

ONE OF THE MOST EXCITING ASPECTS OF THE ILLUSTRATION PROCESS IS TO EXPERIMENT WITH DIFFERENT MEDIA. DIFFERENT COMBINATIONS OF MATERIALS CAN BE USED TO CREATE EXCITING POSSIBILITIES.

One of the techniques available is collage, which is created by overlaying and mixing different materials and then gluing them to a flat surface. But there are also a variety of traditional painting and drawing techniques that involve combining different elements, thus mixing media.

BASIC EQUIPMENT Most illustrators naturally collect inspirational material, such as photographs, different papers, dried leaves, seeds, pasta, string, and all sorts of miscellaneous matter that catches their eye. This reference material is then stored or a mental note made for future use. It is a very good habit to adopt especially if you wish to work in collage.

As collage relies on the reliable fixing of a variety of materials to a surface, you will need a really strong adhesive. The glue that is most appropriate for this technique is PVA (polyvinyl acetate), a white craft glue, because it is both strong and invisible when it dries. It is also important to use an appropriate support for the materials used in the collage. For cut paper, ordinary typing paper is fine, but for more three-dimensional work with heavier materials, you will need a stronger support such as board or card.

The illustrator does not usually set out to create artwork using mixed media. The use of mixed media is more likely to come from a need to produce a particular effect or idea beyond the capabilities of one particular medium.

APPLICATIONS FOR THE ILLUSTRATOR Collage and mixed media are popular techniques for editorial illustration. The only restriction when working in collage concerns the method of reproduction. For instance, a collage using three-dimensional objects, such as seed heads, cannot be reproduced with a drum scanner, so it is advisable to check the method of reproduction to be used.

GETTING STARTED One of the most popular materials for collage is cut paper. You can use layers of colored tissue paper, which are semi-transparent and can be superimposed in a similar way to washes of watercolor. The paper can either be cut with scissors or torn into shape. Collage was first used extensively by the Cubists in Paris at the beginning of the 20th century. They integrated typography cut from newspapers into their paintings. But your composition could include cloth, photographs, all kinds of paper, small objects such as pins or bottle tops, anything in fact as long as you can stick or arrange it firmly on the surface chosen. It is worth arranging the image first before gluing it down as this means you can experiment with the composition.

When first attempting to mix different media, restrict yourself to only two or three different media together at one time.

☞
Acrylic; Airbrushing; Colored Pencils; Gouache; Linework; Markers; Masking Techniques; Pastels.

Use heavyweight paper or illustration board and try to plan your composition and use of mediums before you start. This will help you to achieve a more convincing illustration style and not a rather confused mess.

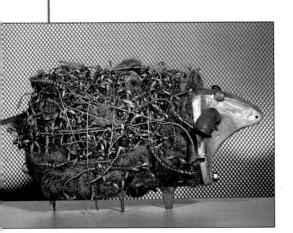

Sophie Marsham
In this illustration collage is combined with sculpture. The artist uses metallic objects to create a three-dimensional image.

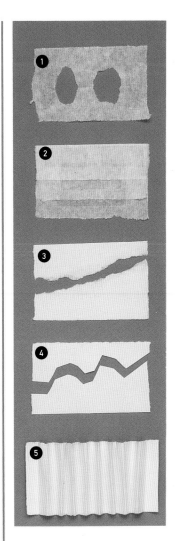

ACRYLIC AND OIL PASTEL

Once you have mastered the basic techniques, there is a whole new range of effects that can be achieved by mixing traditional media together. For an illustrator, it is very important to find a distinctive style, similar to a personal signature. A style can be based on drawing technique and special use of media.

2 When the pastel is laid down and blended, the acrylic wash is still visible underneath. This gives the pastel a textural appearance, very different than a single layer of pastel.

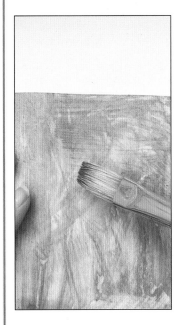

1 This example combines acrylic paint used as a background and oil pastel, which is built up over the top. The acrylic is applied with a large flat brush in bold sketchy strokes. The paint is diluted to allow the paper to show through.

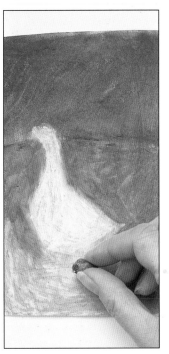

3 The rest of the design is then applied over the acrylic wash, using the same techniques of blending, etc., as for traditional oil pastel.

4 The final design is then fixed to prevent any unintended smudging. A cheaper alternative to manufactured fixative is hair spray.

PAPER EFFECTS

Paper can be manipulated in a range of ways.
1 Torn tissue paper holes.
2 Layered tissue paper.
3 Torn cartridge paper.
4 Cut cartridge paper.
5 Concertinaed cartridge paper.

CUT PAPER

This technique is similar to the ancient art of mosaic, which was used in classical Greece and Rome to decorate the floors and walls of villas. It has become a very popular technique for producing decorative illustrations and is used particularly on wine labels and in food magazines.

2 | For more difficult areas, the design can be drawn on layout paper and then stuck to the mosaic paper with small drops of glue. Cut through both layers to obtain accurate shapes.

1 | The design is drawn out onto the base paper. The other papers are cut to size with either a scalpel or scissors and then stuck down.

3 | Try to keep the design as simple as possible — cutting tiny details can be very time-consuming and ineffective. The glues most appropriate for this method are the ones that dry clear, so that any residue will not show on the finished work.

COLLAGE

Collage has become fashionable in the last few years and is popular with illustrators since it allows them to show off their creativity in both two- and three-dimensional work. One consideration is that most clients will expect you to produce a transparency of the work for reproduction purposes. This means paying a photographer or doing the job yourself. The latter is best as you will have more control over the result. This project shows how fabric, paper, and paint can be combined in a collage.

Working with fabric

Collage is a treat for the squirrels and magpies among us, as it allows an excuse for collecting all kinds of interesting bits and pieces. Fabric is a particularly useful material to collect, the more textured and crumpled the better. Here it is used for the collage background, but whole works can be made in fabric.

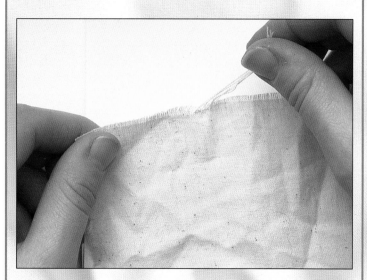

1 | To give your material interesting edges as well as color and texture, the loose threads can be pulled out, leaving a fringe. The more you pull out, the longer the fringe.

Working with paper
A huge variety of handmade papers are available from all around the world which make excellent materials for collage. Try to collect as many scraps of paper as possible, even old brown paper is useful. Keep photographs from magazines, postcards, bus tickets—anything made from paper.

2 | Don't try to smooth out the creases; they give more texture to the work. This piece of canvas is to be used as the background, so it is glued onto a piece of stiff card with either PVA craft glue, or wood glue, which dry clear.

3 | The same fringed effect is given to two pieces of sacking which are in turn glued to the canvas. The idea is to create different areas of texture achieving a layered effect.

2 | Use other photocopies of work free from copyright such as old maps and try out the design before gluing it in place. As with the photo, the edges are torn to soften them.

1 | If your collage is to be published, make sure you don't infringe copyright laws. If you use photographs, as in this collage, it is best to take your own. Use a black and white photocopy, which is thinner than a photograph and can be painted. Tearing around the image creates an interesting edge.

3 | To help blend together and integrate the different materials and also soften hard edges, handmade tissue paper is torn into thin strips and glued around the edges. As it is semi-transparent, it softens the area underneath.

Using paint

Once the glue has dried thoroughly, a process which can be speeded up with a hairdryer, color can be added. The most suitable paint is acrylic, as it is flexible and can be used either opaque or diluted in thin transparent washes. Gold and silver gouache can also be used to great effect.

Building up layers

A major part of the appeal of collage is the visual density that can be achieved by building up successive layers of varying materials.

1 | After the paper is applied, more fabric is added. Gauze (muslin) is very effective as it is soft, semi-translucent, and can be easily "sculpted."

1 | To enhance the texture of the fabric, apply thick paint with a dry brush so that only the tops of the folds receive the color.

2 | Once the darker paint has dried on the fabric, white painted highlights can be added to the very tops of the folds, which emphasizes the three-dimensional effect.

2 | Spread the glue over the background and press on the moistened fabric. The fabric is glued down in folds to give a complex textured effect and this means you can soften edges.

MODELING 3-D IMAGES

Because an illustration can be photographed before it is printed, an increasingly popular form involves three-dimensional objects. These can be gleaned from your "found" collection or, if you need specific objects, they can be made from modeling clay.

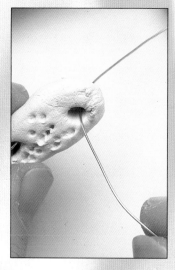

4 | Once all the glue and paint have dried on the layers of paper and fabric, the backing can be removed. This allows the fringe to be used effectively.

2 | Allow the clay to dry thoroughly. Then join the pieces together with thread or wire. The textured marks were made with the brush end.

5 | The final result needs to be carefully photographed, with particular attention to lighting, as this could make or break the effect of your collage. So a collage artist needs to be a photographer as well.

1 | Any form of modeling material can be used, even flour mixed with water. Here, the parts of a crab are molded by hand from quick-drying modeling clay. You can also use cutters for a cleaner effect. The end of a paint brush can be very useful for making holes—here for jointing the crab.

3 | Color is then added using diluted acrylic paint. This is left to dry and then highlights of acrylic gold are added with a dry brush to accentuate the texture.

Colored pencils

COLORED PENCILS ARE AN IDEAL MEDIUM FOR QUICK VISUALIZATIONS AND COLOR APPLICATION, AND THEY ARE A POPULAR MEDIUM FOR BOOK ILLUSTRATION. BECAUSE THEY ARE EASY TO CARRY, THEY ARE IDEAL FOR SKETCHING AND COLLECTING IDEAS.

Any application of pigment to a ground relies on the roughness and texture of the surface. The simplest medium using this technique is the graphite or colored pencil. A range of colored pencils can produce a variety of linear marks using different angles and pressures. Colors can also be mixed using optical techniques such as stippling or hatching. Textured papers will alter the effect, too.

BASIC EQUIPMENT Colored pencils can be bought in sets or singly. They vary in hardness and texture between manufacturers, and it is worth asking to try them out. Water-soluble colors can be used with water to expand the range of techniques available. Turpentine, too, can be applied with a brush to drawings done with high-quality colored pencils.

Your choice of paper will greatly affect your line and style. The surface of paper is made up of a network of long interlocking fibers which act like sandpaper, wearing away at the pigment and trapping it in its web-like structure. Your choice of paper depends on the style of work intended. For highly detailed illustration, a smooth paper with a Hot Press surface is recommended. For a looser, sketchier approach, a rougher or NOT (i.e. NOT Hot Press) paper is more suitable.

APPLICATIONS FOR THE ILLUSTRATOR The main characteristic of colored pencil is its softness, making it ideal for creating moods and suitable for all subjects. Colored pencil is a fashionable technique and is found illustrating cook books, and on greeting cards, as well as in quick visualizations in brochures.

GETTING STARTED For the beginner, colored pencils are an easy medium to use. They have the potential, however, for more involved techniques, and it may take a little time to produce a convincing illustration style.

The basic design can be drawn in graphite pencil, as colored pencils are difficult to erase. If your colored pencils are too hard, they will create indentations which will interfere with the image, and may produce white lines in an area of solid color. To produce a range of tones, use a variety of pressures, or layer colors one over the other, creating an optical mix. It is important to build up the layers slowly, depositing the color evenly. However, there comes a point when it is impossible for the paper to take any more pigment. Tonal changes can also be achieved by hatching and cross-hatching, using one or more colors at different angles.

☞

Collage and Mixed Media; Corrections; Enlarging and Scaling up; Linework; Masking Techniques; Tracing and Transferring.

Solvents are applied with a brush, mixing colors into a wash. You can then work into this wash with further linear marks. Work with speed and confidence, to prevent the colors from becoming muddied by overworking.

Stephen Hall
This detail demonstrates the intensity of color that can be achieved with the medium of watercolor colored pencils.

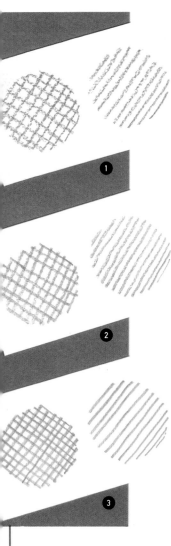

OPTICAL MIXING

This is a traditional method for using colored pencils. This technique works like a color photograph (an arrangement of small colored dots) because the rough texture of the paper breaks up each application of color. When one color is laid over the other, the eye reads it as a mixture of the two separate colors.

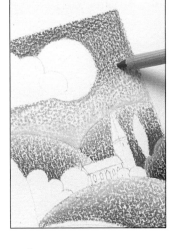

2 | Repeat this technique with each colored area in the illustration. By varying the concentration of the darker "wash," you can control the mix, expressing transitional tones and shadows, and giving the impression of three-dimensionality.

1 | This technique works best using highly textured papers. The outline is first sketched in lightly with a pencil. Each section uses only two colors, a lighter "wash," here yellow, applied first, with the darker one, here green, added over the top.

3 | You may find that pencil pigment comes away from the paper and could mark the illustration if it is not removed. This can be done with a hairdryer or, as in the example, with a large soft brush.

4 | This method is not particularly suited to fine detail, and a successful outcome relies on a simple ordered design. Simplify your shapes, reduce detail, and stick to a limited palette of colors.

PAPER TEXTURES

A heavy texture breaks up the pencil stroke to create a grainy effect. On a smooth paper, the color can be applied more solidly.
Colored-pencil hatching on:
❶ Rough paper.
❷ Not paper.
❸ Hot-pressed paper.

SCRATCHING OUT

It is not always easy to predict where you will need areas of white, so this technique allows you to replace highlights and small light details once the illustration is complete.

WATER-SOLUBLE COLORED PENCIL

Water-soluble colored pencils can be used like any other pencils, but the pigment is softer and can be dissolved with an application of water, leading to some interesting effects. For very wet effects, use watercolor paper, as in this example.

1 | Sketch out the design with a pencil and then add the colored pencil, being aware that the water added in the last stage will soften edges and merge tones and colors.

2 | The pencil is applied in a similar way to the optical mixing technique (see p.35), but in this illustration a greater number of colors have been superimposed.

Water-soluble pencils (opposite, top) must be a separate purchase as traditional colored pencils (below) do not mix with water.

| Here a soft reflection is needed on the peach. A sharp scalpel is used to scratch away the pigment by gently dragging the blade across the paper in one direction. Repeat until enough of the pencil has been removed to return the paper to white.

3 With the application of color complete, the water can be applied. Traditionally this is done with a brush, focusing on certain areas of the illustration. In this case a plant spray is used, producing an overall softening of the image. The illustration is laid flat and the spray held approximately 6 in. (15 cm) away. Continue spraying until the colors have merged to your satisfaction.

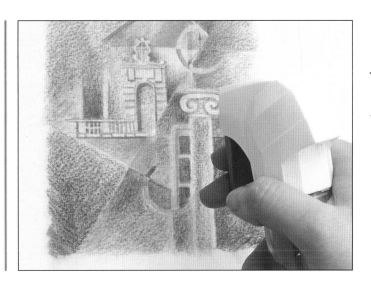

4 As the water was applied in a spray, the effect is subtle and the finished illustration keeps some of the sharpness of the original design.

SOLVENTS

Colored pencils can also be smudged and blended using a variety of other solvents, including turpentine and lighter fluid. These can be used on traditional colored pencils, enabling you to achieve a wide range of effects.

Here lighter fluid is brushed over colored pencil to create a softly blended effect without entirely losing the texture.

Color-separated artwork

AN INEXPENSIVE ROUTE TO COLOR REPRODUCTION AND THEREFORE A USEFUL EXPERTISE FOR THE ILLUSTRATOR, COLOR-SEPARATED ARTWORK IS A LITTLE COMPLICATED TO MASTER, BUT EXCITING RESULTS CAN BE OBTAINED WITH THE HELP OF A GOOD PRINTER.

Although the illustrator designs the image and the separate sheets of color, the final work is assembled in the course of the printing process. If you look at a magazine color illustration with a magnifying glass, you will see that it is made up of minute dots of color: yellow, red (magenta), blue (cyan), and black. The percentages of each color can be varied in relation to the others, creating a whole range of colors. This is a relatively expensive process. A cheaper method is to separate the colors at the illustration stage with color-separated artwork.

BASIC EQUIPMENT The most important material needed for this technique is dimensionally stable paper. Dimensionally stable paper is specifically manufactured not to react to any moisture, either from ink or the atmosphere. If the illustration were to be executed on paper that could be affected by moisture, and then stretched, this would change the eventual printed result. As the artwork is produced on separate sheets, any variations in registration (the marking of each sheet to ensure the exact positioning of one sheet over the other) can cause a change in the printed image. Other materials include different-sized brushes, good-quality black waterproof ink, color key film, and a scalpel for cutting it.

APPLICATIONS FOR THE ILLUSTRATOR The mastery of color separation is a useful addition to any illustrator's portfolio, as it means artwork can be used for large print runs at a much reduced cost per finished illustration. It is often used for packaging, such as milk cartons and plastic bags.

GETTING STARTED Do not be deterred by the technical nature of this process. It is much easier than it sounds and is also very enjoyable.

Before any separation work is undertaken, it is helpful first to produce a rough drawing to use as a template, showing the positions of the separate colors. The individual sheets, showing where each color will appear, are then executed with reference to this master. All artwork is rendered in black ink, with tonal work added in line or color key film, which is a sheet of fine dots of varying sizes that are transferred by rubbing with a blunt stylus. It is important to include approximately 1/8 in. (3 mm) of bleed (extra image or overlap). This will prevent any gaps from occurring between colors when they are printed. It is vital that each separate sheet is carefully marked with registration marks. Do this before you start each new sheet and check them occasionally to make sure they have not moved position while you have been working on the illustration.

With this method, the illustrator can choose to restrict the choice of colors used, i.e. just black and cyan, which would further reduce the price of reproduction.

☞
Computer Illustration;
Enlarging and Scaling up;
Linework.

PREPARING ARTWORK

As this is an involved process that brings together many separate pieces of artwork in creating the final image, it is vital to register each sheet accurately. Use dimensionally stable (D/S) paper thereby ensuring against any inaccuracies in registration caused by moist atmosphere.

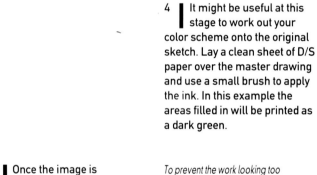

2 | The master drawing is then traced from the original sketch. In this example a dip pen was used with waterproof India ink. Dimensionally stable paper has a smooth surface which is wonderful for fine line work.

4 | It might be useful at this stage to work out your color scheme onto the original sketch. Lay a clean sheet of D/S paper over the master drawing and use a small brush to apply the ink. In this example the areas filled in will be printed as a dark green.

To prevent the work looking too mechanical, try to keep your lines as expressive as possible.

3 | Once the image is complete and absolutely dry, the registration marks can be added. In most cases only three registration points are necessary, placed as far apart as possible and well away from the printing image.

1 | Creating the image is the first step. This can be done with pencil on layout paper. Make sure the image is dark enough to show through the dimensionally stable paper which is similar to tracing paper but is heavier.

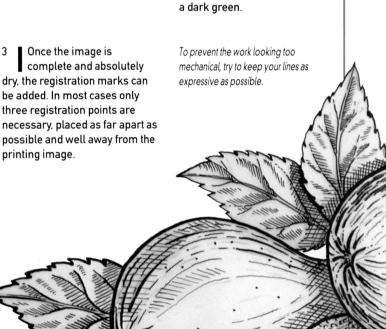

5 | As each new sheet of paper is added, make sure that the registration marks are accurately traced through before starting the inking in. Each sheet defines the areas to be printed in each separate color.

MATCHING PANTONE COLORS

The Pantone color system is made for designers, printers, or anyone working with color. It works by identifying over 500 colors by a number. This allows the illustrator to specify a color to the printer.

1 | When all the pages are separated, making sure each sheet has registration marks, a small square of the Pantone color, (which includes the number) is then taped to each sheet.

6 | Although the colors are rendered in black they will be eventually printed in your chosen Pantone color. As each layer is added, the whole image will gradually fill in until the only areas left will be those you wish to leave white.

2 | The final image is then created by the printer. Each individual color is overlaid one on top of the other, using black for the key outline. This is where accurate registration is vital, if done badly you will end up with unwanted areas of white, or superimposed colors.

Computer illustration

THE COMPUTER IS BECOMING

INCREASINGLY POPULAR IN THE

CONTEXT OF ILLUSTRATION.

Most artists who move on to work with computers have had some experience experimenting with traditional media in various ways; computer illustration is really no different. Although the idea may initially seem daunting to those accustomed to using more traditional methods, most of the major software packages are user-friendly, and once you have seen the results they can achieve, may rapidly become addictive.

The regular tools which you would expect from a paint-and-draw package— for example, airbrush, pencil, paint-and-fill options —are constantly being improved and expanded as software becomes more highly developed, with new features introduced and old ones updated. One of these features is the layers option, which allows you to edit, paste, and add effects to one layer (presuming you are working with several), without disturbing the rest of the image. Filters can also be used. These allow you to create many fascinating effects with minimum effort, including making ripples, embossing, and blurring.

The three main pieces of equipment required for creating illustrations in this way are, first, a personal computer, second, the relevant software packages, and third, a scanning device to scan in your raw material. Flat-bed scanners usually give the best results, but hand-held scanners are adequate. The equipment is perhaps the major drawback to the technique, as the initial outlay for equipment can be considerable. For the beginner it might be advisable to begin by approaching someone who has the correct hardware and software and will allow you to experiment with the techniques before deciding whether to purchase your own.

A computer-generated image is usually begun by collecting a series of relevant pictures to work with, the choice depending on the subject matter you have in mind. Personal photographs are a good starting point, and copyright-free images from a stock library can also be very useful. Once you have collected your images, and have access to a scanner, the next step is to download your images onto your computer's hard disk. You are then ready to begin the creative process, using all the tools and effects available. Always bear in mind, however, that composition is the major ingredient for success, as in any illustration.

Peter Gudynas
This is an example of the variety of effects possible with modern computer software packages. Original images have been scanned into the computer and manipulated using effects such as layering and filters. The artist has used a selection of manipulated photographs, creating a complex composition that communicates an instant sensation. Truly electronic art for an electronic age.

TOOLS

Computer illustration is similar to any other illustration technique in that you have to master the tools before you can then move on to the techniques. Shown here are some of the tools that can be used to add special touches. These, which appear in a pull-down menu or "tool box," allow you to select, paint, edit, and view images, and to choose and control the foreground and background colors.

Overlaying colors with hard and soft edges.

Airbrush with large spray option Allows color fill over a larger area.

Blending of colors in a linear left to right movement.

Circular gradient over an aqua background.

❶ *Gradient tool*
Used for filling large areas, allowing you to apply either a radial or straight transition from the foreground to the background color.

Paintbrush creates the same effects as a traditional paintbrush.

Creating a filled color area by overlapping the edges of each line.

Overlaying a variety of transparent colors using an opacity of 45%.

A textured effect using the airbrush tool.

❷ *Airbrush tool*
Allows you to lay down a diffused layer of paint on top of the image you are working on. It is especially good for tidying rough edges.

Tartan effect over a navy blue background.

❸ *Paintbrush tool*
This can be used to create soft edges freehand, in any color and with a variety of different-sized brushes.

Line tool creates a line similar to a pencil or pen, with a hard edge.

Line tool has an option that helps you create arrows.

Line tool, showing line thicknesses and direction, in a variety of colors.

❹ *Line tool*
Lets you paint straight, broken or unbroken lines with a variety of brush sizes.

IMAGE MANIPULATION

Manipulating your image can be carried out by using the following techniques and effects: channels and masks, using layers, using filters, resizing, and color correction. Each of these major techniques provides alternative possibilities, for instance there are a whole variety of filters, such as blur filters, which in turn include motion and radial, blur filters, and so on.

❶ The Wind filter creates tiny horizontal lines in the image.
❷ The flowers were rescaled, and the color of each replaced.
❸ The Despeckle filter blurs everything but edges.
❹ The Tiles filter breaks up the image into a series of tiles.

Unmanipulated image
The unmanipulated image is made up of the illustrator's own collection of pictures, cut out and collaged together.

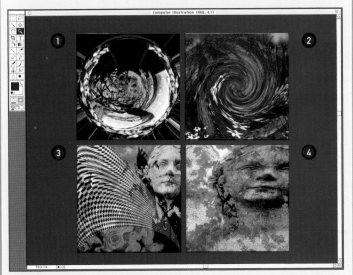

❶ The Posterize command allows you to specify tonal levels.
❷ The original image has been manipulated with the Emboss filter.
❸ The color balance of an image can be adjusted with the Selective Color command or with the Color Balance.
❹ The background has been made darker.

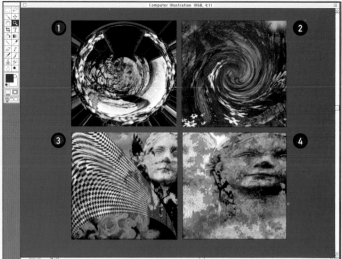

❶ The Crystalize filter clumps pixels into a solid color in a polygon shape. The color has also been replaced.
❷ The Map Invert turns a positive image into a negative.
❸ The Shear filter is used to distort the image along a specified curve.
❹ Converting the image using the Gray scale creates 256 gray shades.

❶ The Pinch filter is used to distort the selection into the center.
❷ The Lens Flair filter simulates a refraction effect.
❸ The Desaturate command reduces the saturation of all colors to 0%.
❹ Posterize allows the specification of the number of tonal values.

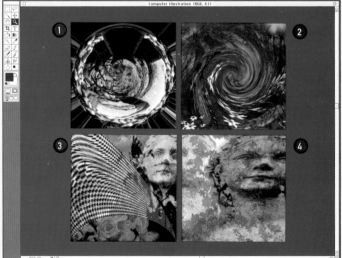

❶ The Graphic Pen filter enhances the line quality of an image.
❷ The background is given a grid effect with the Tile filter.
❸ The Ripple filter is used to produce an undulating pattern.
❹ The Graphic Pen filter was used to emphasize the linear quality.

❶ The Polar Co-ordinates filter distorts the selection.
❷ The Twirl filter rotates the selection around a point in the center.
❸ The Mezzotint filter converts the image into black and white areas.
❹ Selective Color command modifies colors by changing their pigment values.

IMITATING TRADITIONAL MEDIA: *WATERCOLOR*

Once you have mastered the tools available in the various menus, you can then move on to experimenting with the different techniques. With some, you can create completely new effects, but others can successfully imitate traditional media, including watercolor.

3 | A green background color was created on the background layer, or layer one. This can be done by using either the gradient fill or the airbrush tool.

4 | The paintbrush tool was then selected with the wet edges option, and overlapping dots made with a series of yellows, whites, and blacks, to mimic the effect of watercolor.

1 | The artist began by scanning in a photograph of a daffodil. The image was then converted to layers, which put the daffodil into the foreground and pushed the green area into the background.

2 | The image invert was then used to delete the green background altogether, and the daffodil was duplicated three times. To give interest to the image, the flower was reworked and given two different perspectives.

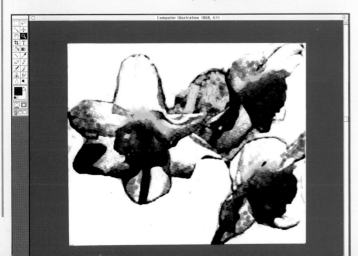

COLLAGE

Collage is a highly creative and versatile medium which allows you to experiment in countless ways. All you need is a bit of imagination, the rest is remarkably simple.

1 | The collection of images to be used for the collage are laid on the scanner, scanned into a new file, and saved.

3 | The tree and snowdrops were then imported and pasted into the second layer, to give the impression that the images disappear behind the first column. A clone tool was used to copy the flowers to increase the number of snowdrops.

4 | The tiled-effect background was then imported into the file and copied into a fourth background layer.

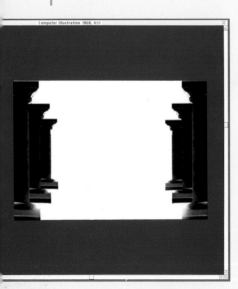

2 | A new file was created in the draw package, and the column was selectively copied and pasted into the foreground and then into a second and third layer. The image was rescaled progressively, so that the columns are larger in the foreground, to give a sense of perspective. The whole image was then copied and flipped horizontally, to achieve a mirrored effect.

5 The pine cone, the next object to be imported, was copied into the foreground, and to further enhance the perspective effect, was copied repeatedly, with the scale and opacity varied.

6 A final fifth layer was created, and the image of the Renaissance lady copied into it, at a slightly reduced percentage of opacity, again adding to the impression of atmospheric perspective.

SEPIA TONE

Using draw packages enables you to give a modern photograph the effect of an old print, changing it from black and white or color to sepia tone. There are two alternative techniques for doing this, described here and on the following page.

Sepia tone: method one

1 The photograph is placed on the scanner and imported into a new file. Then, if the image is color, it is converted to black and white.

2 The duotone function in the mode menu will give you a choice of duotones from the whole color spectrum. For a sepia tone, choose the range of browns. This will automatically apply the tones to your image.

Sepia tone: method two

1 | As before, the first step is to scan and import the photograph into a new file, to copy and paste an image into a new file from an existing one, as in this example.

2 | In this technique, the sepia tone is achieved by changing the tonal range of the original by selecting and replacing the blacks and grays with sepia brown. This can be easily picked from the computer's color circle.

SAVING YOUR WORK

Untitled folder

Once you have finished an image, or even if you just want to take a short break, remember to save your work. You can save an image on the computer's hard disk, a floppy disk, or an external hard drive. First choose "save as," give your document a name, and choose the file format you wish to save it as. "Tiffs," standing for "the tagged-image file format," is the standard, allowing you to exchange documents between applications and other computer platforms. You can also use "Compressed Tiff," which will reduce the overall file size to make better use of disk space.

Winter

PRINTING YOUR IMAGE

Until you can afford a printer of your own you will probably need to go to a specialist bureau to print your work. You will find lists in your local directory. If you take your disk along, they will be able to print out your piece of work in various sizes,

usually for a reasonable price—but do shop around for the best quote. The print shop will be able to advise you on which type of printer will give you the best results; there may be a choice between dye sublimation printers or laser jet printers.

Corrections

ALL OF US, AT SOME TIME OR ANOTHER,

MAKE MISTAKES, BUT BEFORE CRUMPLING

UP YOUR WORK AND GIVING UP IN

DESPAIR, YOU MIGHT TRY SOME OF THE FOLLOWING

HANDY TIPS.

For each medium there are different ways of making corrections. However, often you will not need to make a correction and can adjust your work to include your mistake, or even turn it to your advantage. You can help prevent mistakes by using a clean sheet of scrap paper under your hand to prevent smudging and moisture or grease from spoiling the surface of the paper. Always have a roll of paper towels at hand. Use paper towels as tissue tends to disintegrate too easily. Paper towels can help in a multitude of situations, from mopping up spilt water, to cleaning up edges or removing a too-wet wash.

BASIC EQUIPMENT A most useful piece of equipment for erasable media is the kneaded (putty) eraser, which is far more versatile than an ordinary eraser. It can be molded into a fine point for small detailed areas and it does not leave your work and the studio floor covered in "rubbings out." Also invaluable are white gouache or white correction fluid, an old but clean brush, a scalpel handle and a selection of blades.

APPLICATIONS FOR THE ILLUSTRATOR Learning how to correct work so that it does not show will save the illustrator time and money. The method chosen will depend on the materials used and, most important, the intended use of the illustration. A black and white drawing, for example, can be corrected with white gouache or correction fluid if it is to be reproduced photographically, but for a presentation, some other means would have to be sought.

GETTING STARTED Work using graphite pencil, charcoal, and water-soluble pencil, if the paper is strong enough, can all be erased with a kneaded (putty) eraser, or, if more pressure is needed, a traditional eraser. Scalpel blades can be used to scratch away mistakes made in waterproof inks, wax crayons, and oil pastels.

The blade particularly suitable for this is a size 10, as it has a rounded end to prevent you from cutting the paper. Small areas may also be corrected with white gouache or correcting fluid. It is possible to build up the layers of gouache until the mistake is completely hidden; the only drawback is that it cannot be worked over. For opaque media, making corrections is easy, as the mistake can be worked over once the area is dry.

With water-soluble media, try to dab off the area as quickly as possible, with a piece of paper towel. Next the area can be washed with water applied with an old brush; working at the surface helps the paper give up the pigment. As a last resort, if the illustration is the result of many hours work and the mark still won't come out, or if the area is too dry, a patch can be made so that you can rework the area. This is tricky but can be very effective, as the patch, if it is well made, will be invisible.

MOLDING A KNEADED (PUTTY) ERASER

A useful tip is to keep a kneaded eraser in your pocket to keep it warm. This way it retains its malleability.

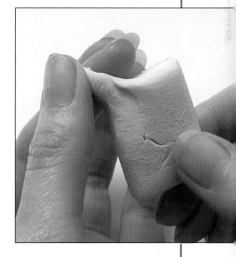

☞
Acrylic; Airbrushing; Brush Drawing; Charcoal; Collage and Mixed Media; Colored Pencils; Gouache; Line and Wash; Linework; Markers; Pastels.

| When a kneaded eraser is brand new, it is quite hard. Before you use it, warm it up in your hand and squeeze it between your fingers. After a while it will soften, enabling you to mold it into a fine point, ideal for erasing small intricate areas. These erasers last a long time if looked after; try not to drop them on the floor, as they pick up dirt and hair very easily.

USING A SCALPEL

A scalpel can be used for corrections in almost any medium. Always make sure that the scalpel blade is clean and sharp. In this demonstration, the illustrator is using a No. 10A blade, which has a pointed end, ideal for removing details. Take care when using this technique on lightweight papers, or you may go through the paper.

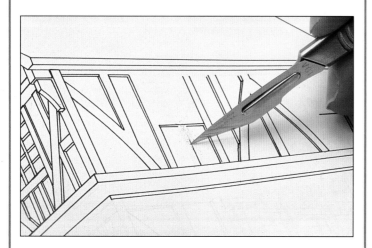

1 A mistake in a technical pen drawing can sometimes be best rectified with a scalpel. Try to scrape the blade in one direction only as this will help prevent the paper surface from roughening.

2 If, when the correction is complete, the paper has roughened, the end of the scalpel, your nail or other smooth, hard, rounded surface can be used to gently burnish the paper fibers flat.

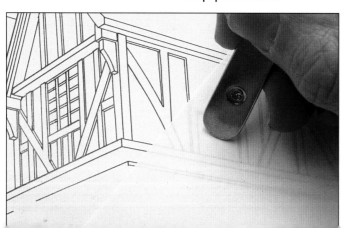

WASHING OUT

This correction technique is suitable only for water-based media, and is particularly suited to watercolor. For best results, it must be attempted as soon as the mistake has been made, before the paint has had time to dry. Drying times vary depending on atmospheric conditions and the type of paper used; more heavily sized papers take longer to dry.

1 As soon as the mistake has happened, dab the area with a clean corner of kitchen paper towel to remove a good quantity of the pigment. Take care not to spread the pigment further by pressing too hard, too quickly.

2 Then, using a clean brush and water, loosen the pigment with small circular strokes. Again, dab the area with paper towel. Continue this process until the painted paper returns to white.

PATCHING

It is not unheard of for a client to ask an illustrator to make fundamental changes to an illustration after it has been completed. At this stage it is often difficult to use some of the easier correction methods, or the surface area may be too large to make them feasible. In these cases, patching is the last resort. It is time-consuming, but you will learn to judge if it is going to save time in the end.

2 | The shape is traced onto a piece of watercolor paper identical to the paper used for the illustration. Then, using a new scalpel blade, cut out the patch.

3 | If the patch were to be superimposed on the illustration as it is, it would create a shadow. To eliminate this problem, the edges of the patch are shaved down with a scalpel. This is done on the BACK of the patch, shaving from the center to the outside edge.

1 | In this example the third cherry is to be completely removed. The first step is to map the area to be patched onto tracing paper.

4 | The patch is then stuck to the illustration using a small amount of glue. When the illustration is reproduced, the camera will not pick up the patch and will read the paper as white. With a perfect patch, which takes practice, it is possible to paint over it as if the mistake had never happened.

Enlarging and scaling up

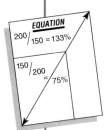

THERE ARE VARIOUS TECHNIQUES USED TO ENLARGE AN IMAGE. IN THE PAST IT WAS A LABORIOUS PROCESS, BUT WITH THE ADVENT OF THE GRANT ENLARGER AND THE PHOTOCOPIER, IT CAN NOW TAKE SIMPLY THE CLICK OF A BUTTON.

You can enlarge or reduce an image in a number of ways, manually or mechanically. The manual method uses a squared grid system which is an effective technique for enlarging simple sketches. Mechanical methods include the Grant projector, used by designers for accurately traced scaled pictorial images. A projector is an extremely useful piece of equipment for large-scale work, but perhaps the most accessible method of enlarging is the photocopier.

BASIC EQUIPMENT Most of the mechanical equipment for enlarging is extremely expensive, although it is possible these days to find a good, inexpensive photocopying service not too far away. Grant enlargers and projectors can be bought more reasonably priced second-hand, but cannot compare with the bargain price of the grid method, which uses only a pencil and ruler.

APPLICATIONS FOR THE ILLUSTRATOR It is often necessary for an illustrator to enlarge an image because most artwork is reproduced larger than the printed image. Using these mechanical methods saves valuable time redrawing the original image. They can also be useful for enlarging reference material, making it easier to work from. The manual method is always available to you for simple illustrations or when the mechanical equipment breaks down.

GETTING STARTED Two grids are used for the manual method, one on the reference image and a smaller or larger one on the paper you are transferring the image to. The grid is made up of squares which can be numbered to help identification. The major points are then plotted from the reference image onto the larger grid and then joined up, trying to reproduce the flow of the original line.

The Grant projector has an illuminated adjustable-height table on which the illustration is placed. The image is then projected onto a horizontal ground-glass table. This image can then be focused and enlarged or reduced, and traced onto thin paper such as tracing or layout paper. A slide projector can also be used if you want to enlarge an image considerably. A transparency, or an original study on film, can be projected onto paper. It is necessary to stand to one side while tracing the outline so as not to obscure the image.

Perhaps the easiest method of producing an enlarged or reduced image is to use a photocopier. This machine uses percentages to gauge the scale, thus 100% is the same size as the original, 150% is half as large again, and 50% is half the size of the original. The simple rule for working out the amount of enlargement is, "divide what you want by what you have got." So if your illustration is 6 inches (15cm) wide and you want it enlarged to 8 inches (20 cm), follow the advice and divide 8 by 6 which equals $\frac{8}{6} = 1\frac{1}{3} = 133\%$.

☞

Tracing and Transferring.

ENLARGING AND SCALING UP

Before the invention of the photocopier there were many ingenious inventions designed to help the artist enlarge and reduce simple outlines, some more successful than others. It is worth knowing some of the methods since you may not always have access to a photocopier.

GRID METHOD

This is perhaps one of the simplest methods, one that you may have learned at school. It can be used for everything from simple sketches to more detailed work.

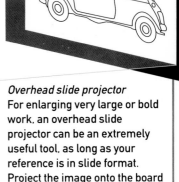

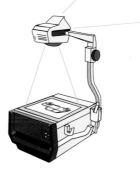

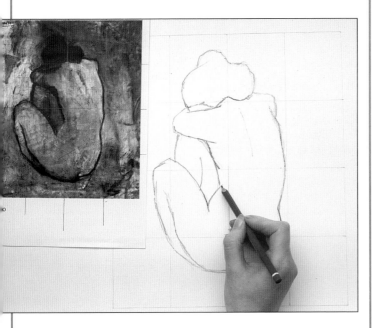

Overhead slide projector
For enlarging very large or bold work, an overhead slide projector can be an extremely useful tool, as long as your reference is in slide format. Project the image onto the board or canvas in a darkened room, and trace around the projected image.

Grant enlarger
These are bulky, heavy machines, and are consequently not suitable for the small studio. The machine works by magnifying an original image. The piece to be enlarged is placed on a flat metal shelf,

which can be raised or lowered to change the degree of enlargement. This shelf is below the viewing screen, onto which is placed your paper. A bright light illuminates the image, making it possible to trace the enlargement.

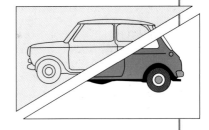

Using a pencil and ruler, draw a grid of horizontal and vertical lines lightly onto the image you wish to copy . Then repeat the grid on a separate sheet, either enlarging or reducing the size of the squares, depending on whether you wish to enlarge or reduce the image. Work out a series of key points on the original image and then transfer those points onto the new grid. You will end up with a series of dots which you will then join together. The more complicated the image, the greater the number of dots you will need to draw.

Etching

A POPULAR PRINT-MAKING TECHNIQUE SINCE THE SIXTEENTH CENTURY, ETCHING IS STILL HARD TO BEAT FOR HIGH-QUALITY PRINT MAKING, BUT ECONOMICS HAVE RESTRICTED ITS USE.

Etching is a printing technique where a metal plate is coated with a wax-based substance, which is worked on with an etching needle to expose the metal beneath. The plate is then dipped in acid which bites into the plate where it is exposed, producing an "engraved" plate ready for inking and printing.

BASIC EQUIPMENT The beginner will learn to etch under supervision where the basic equipment required will be provided. You will need a copper, steel or zinc plate; an acid-resistant wax-based substance called a ground; stopping-out varnish; an etching needle; a tray made of glass, porcelain or enamel, or a plastic photographic tray; and finally an acid, either Dutch mordant, nitric acid or ferric chloride. Each of the three acids have different "biting" times, and can be used to create different effects.

The grounds used for etching are referred to as soft or hard. A hard ground is made from beeswax, bitumen and rosin. Soft grounds use the same recipe, but are mixed with tallow or grease. Both grounds can be bought in either solid or liquid form.

Stopping-out varnish is acid-resistant; it is used as added protection for areas not to be etched and for the back and sides of the plate. The etching needle has an extremely fine point, which is not too sharp, as the intention is to draw into the ground, not to scratch the metal.

APPLICATIONS FOR THE ILLUSTRATOR This technique was used extensively in the past to illustrate books. Its use these days is restricted to fine art printing because it is labor intensive and expensive to set up.

GETTING STARTED The difference between etching and engraving is that the engraved line is cut into the metal itself, whereas in etching it is drawn into the acid-resistant ground, and the acid is then left to "engrave" the line. An etched line can have more depth, width and texture than an engraved one.

To prepare for etching, the plate is first covered with a thin film of either soft or hard ground. The back and sides have also to be protected with varnish. Using the etching needle, the composition is drawn into the ground, exposing the metal. The plate is then immersed in an acid bath, where the exposed metal is etched into by the acid. Using stopping-out varnish on already exposed lines, it is possible to return the plate into the bath to further etch certain lines. This process can be repeated as many times as you wish.

Finally the plate is removed from the bath and the ground and varnish is removed with mineral (white) spirits. The plate is warmed before ink is dabbed over the surface, making sure that all the lines are filled. The excess is then wiped off and the plate is positioned on the press with the printing paper on top. Thus the first impression may be made.

Glynn Thomas
The yellow-green predominant in this charming composition gives a sunny, bright tone to the image, with the contrast of brown and dark green contributing space and depth.

Enlarging and Scaling up; Linework; Linoleumcut and Woodcut; Tracing and Transferring.

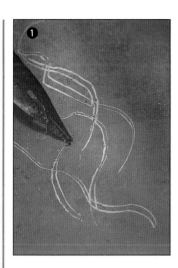

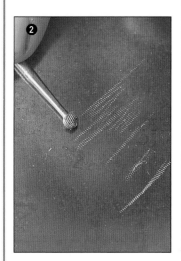

ALTERNATIVE TOOLS

You can use a purpose-made etching needle to improvise with a darning needle attached firmly to a pen or brush handle.

❶ An ordinary dip pen makes calligraphic, double lines because of the split in the nib.
❷ A small roulette—this is a dentist's drill bit—rolled over the ground makes a lightly toothed liner pattern.

PREPARING THE PLATE

Before you start, make sure you are equipped with all the materials you will need. The basic equipment for etching consists of a metal plate (copper or zinc), an acid-resistant ground and varnish, an etching needle, an acid bath, printing paper, ink, and an etching press.

The usual choice of metal for the plate is either zinc or copper, the former perhaps more suitable for the beginner as it is less expensive. The plate must then be carefully prepared. Remove the sharp outer edges, which can cut the paper when printing, and clean any grease from the plate.

Beveling the plate

1 | This process can be done either as a preliminary one, or immediately before printing. Angle a file at 45 degrees to the plate; hold the plate firmly with one edge protruding from the bench and file the edge into a 45-degree angle. Repeat this process on all sides of the plate.

2 | Usually the file will leave the edge a little rough, so to give a smoother finish, work the edges with a scraper held at the same angle.

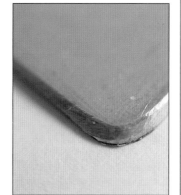

3 | Because the plate is pressed deep into the surface of the paper during printing, sharp edges would cut into the paper. The pressure also leaves a clear impression of the edges of the plate on the paper. A different effect can be obtained by rounding off the corners of the plate completely.

Degreasing

1 | If the plate is not cleaned completely, the ground will not stick properly to the surface, which means the non-printing areas will print badly. Start by mixing a small amount of French chalk with a few drops of ammonia on the surface of the plate.

2 | Using a small scrubbing brush, rag or absorbent cotton (cotton wool), work the ammonia and chalk across the whole surface of the plate.

3 | When a plate which is completely free of grease is rinsed with clean water, the water will run evenly off the surface, rather than collecting around grease spots. Repeat Step 2 if any grease remains.

Etching grounds come in a solid cake form, and are made from beeswax, bitumen, and resin. They can be bought in two types, hard and soft: hard for line etching; soft to create surface effects on the plate.

APPLYING HARD GROUND

The ground acts as a resistant coat that protects the plate from the acid. It must therefore be applied evenly, which will also help it lift cleanly when you draw into it with the etching needle. The ground, made of bitumen, wax, and rosin, is bought as a solid ball and must be melted before it can be applied.

1 | Warm the prepared plate through on a hotplate. Dab the ball of ground onto the surface, allowing it to melt leaving random smears. Be careful; if you overheat the ground, it will not adhere evenly.

2 | Working in all directions, spread the ground evenly over the plate with a roller. Applying the ground accurately is a matter of practice. If it becomes lumpy, cool the plate, clean off the ground, and start again.

3 | The ultimate goal is to achieve a uniform, thin, even, golden-brown coat by continuing to work the roller from side to side in both directions on the plate.

Smoking

4 | This step is not essential, but it can help harden the ground and blacken the surface, which makes it easier to see where you have drawn into the ground. Hold the edge of the plate with a pair of pliers, protecting it from scratching with a folded piece of paper. Light a thick twist of three or four tapers, which will give a long flame. Allow the smoke to touch only the ground, and move the flame until the ground is uniformly dark.

At various stages of the etching technique, the plate is worked with heat, therefore safety factors must be a priority.

DRAWING ON THE PLATE

The most important thing to remember is that you are not trying to draw into the metal, only to lift the ground. Draw with the etching needle in much the same way that you would use a pencil or pen, but you do not have to lift away all the ground down to the surface of the metal.

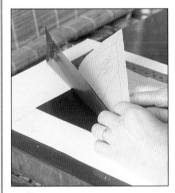

1 If you are nervous of drawing freehand onto the plate, use transfer paper to trace your design onto the plate.

2 Tape the sketch, with the transfer paper underneath, down firmly onto the plate or cardboard frame. Try not to press too hard as this may damage the surface of the ground.

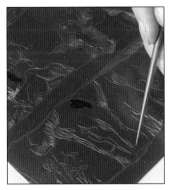

3 The delight of etching is exploiting the characteristics of the materials and the printing methods, so when drawing freehand try to let the composition and line quality reflect this.

Stopping out

4 Stopping-out varnish also protects the plate from the acid. When the drawing is complete, paint stopping-out varnish onto any areas where the ground is imperfect. Include the edges and back of the plate, making sure that no bare metal except the image is exposed to the acid.

BITING THE PLATE

Unfortunately, there are no simple rules to help you judge how long the plate needs to be immersed in acid. Many factors can vary the strength of the "bite" of the acid, including the type of metal and acid used, the temperature of the acid, and the amount of metal left exposed.

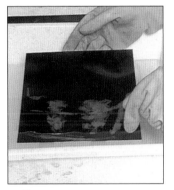

1 When you place the plate in the acid bath, make sure you lower it gently and wear gloves to prevent any contact with the acid. The line will change the longer you leave the plate in the acid.

2 As the reaction takes place between the plate and the acid, little bubbles will appear. Brush them away gently with a feather.

3 When the acid has completed its job, remove the plate and wash the acid away under running water.

4 To remove the ground and the stopping-out varnish, wipe the plate with mineral spirits (white spirit). The first proof can now be taken from the plate.

Gouache

GOUACHE OFFERS THE ILLUSTRATOR ENORMOUS FLEXIBILITY AS IT COMBINES THE SOLUBILITY AND TRANSLUCENCY OF WATERCOLOR WITH THE OPAQUE QUALITIES OF HEAVIER PAINTS. IT REPRODUCES WELL.

pale areas, use the white of the paper, as in watercolor, to shine through thin washes, or add white to your mix and superimpose it over dark.

Gouache remains more soluble than watercolor when it is dry, making it easier to manipulate and blend when superimposing new layers. It is possible to overlay opaque layers over transparent and vice versa.

This water-based medium is ideal for producing large areas of flat, even color which can be worked over when dry, enabling you to add extra detail and form. It can be laid down in thin washes or built up in thicker opaque layers from dark to light. Gouache is often the preferred medium for airbrushing since the pigment is finely ground.

BASIC EQUIPMENT Gouache is thicker and more flexible than watercolor. It contains more binder and has added white pigment, making it opaque at full strength. What determines the quality, and consequently the price, of the different makes is the quality of the pigments. Gouache has a smooth texture which reproduces well. The opaque nature of these paints means they can be painted onto colored papers as well as the usual range of thicker cartridge used for watercolor. The choice of brushes is also similar to those used for watercolor.

GETTING STARTED Gouache is considered easier for the beginner to master than watercolor. It can be worked, rather like watercolor, in thin washes, or superimposed in opaque layers, from dark to light, similar to acrylics or oils. To darken colors, superimpose further layers of the same color with less water, and to achieve

☞

Acrylic; Airbrushing; Brush Drawing; Collage and Mixed Media; Colored Pencils; Corrections; Linework; Monoprint; Resist Techniques; Watercolor.

Debbie Ryder
Blending one color into another can be achieved in a number of ways with gouache. In this illustration the artist has used blocks of color that butt up to one another.

DIFFERENT EFFECTS

Depending on the type of paper used, the results achievable with gouache paint can vary quite dramatically. Gouache paint can be used either neat from the tube or in watered-down washes. The more water that is added to a wash the more translucent the pigment becomes and the thinner the paint; the thinner the wash the more paper texture shows through.

❶ Hot-pressed paper with (from left to right): wet wash; medium wash; from the tube.
❷ Cold-pressed paper with: wet wash; medium wash; from the tube.
❸ Rough paper: wet wash; medium wash; straight from the tube.

OPAQUE COLOR

This method of using gouache is possibly the simplest and takes advantage of its individual properties. The amount of water added to the pigment affects the opacity of the paint: the more water you add, the more transparent it becomes.

1 First draw the outline of the design lightly in pencil using a 140lb./300gsm NOT surface paper and a No. 3 sable brush. The gouache paint is mixed with water until it is the consistency of light (single) cream.

2 Starting at the top and working down, fill each area with a flat wash. If when dry you find the wash is patchy, you will have added too much water. Don't worry; mix the same color with a little less water and go over the same area again.

3 | When the first wash is completely dry, the shadow colors can be added. Apply the paint with confidence; if you are too fiddly, you may disturb the first wash so that the two colors mix.

4 | The finished illustration shows the solidity of color possible with gouache. It reproduces successfully and is particularly suited to stylized work.

OPAQUE AND TRANSLUCENT WASHES

Gouache can be combined in thick, opaque washes superimposed into thinner, translucent layers. For this illustration use 140lb./300gsm NOT watercolor paper and sable brushes.

1 | After the outline has been completed in pencil, an opaque wash is applied. Try to work quickly so that the wash is worked very wet. It will then dry to an even surface.

2 | Once the opaque wash has dried, the thinner translucent washes can be applied on top. The paint is mixed until it is quite runny; this mixing can be done on the illustration. Work quickly so as not to disturb the opaque wash beneath. Some mixing is desirable.

3 Fine detail can be added after the washes with a fine felt-tip pen. Do not use a dip pen and ink, as the ink will bleed into the paint.

4 When all the washes are dry, other detail can be added with thick gouache, as can be seen in the stars in this illustration. Modeling and shadows are rendered in thin washes, such as the creamy shadow on the cow.

IMPASTO

This technique is probably more effective if you are working with acrylic paint, but using gouache can also be successful. The paint is used as it comes out of the tube. Do not add extra water as the consistency will be lighter, which will detract from the impasto effect.

1 Here, the background area has been applied first in flat gouache to enhance the impasto effect. The orange paint is then applied as thickly as possible. Try to create as much surface texture as you can with the brush.

2 In this example two colors —red and yellow—were mixed on the paper, which strengthens the impasto effect.

Line and wash

THE LINE AND WASH TECHNIQUE ALLOWS THE ARTIST TO CREATE A COMPLETE IMAGE EXTREMELY QUICKLY. IT HAS BEEN THE PREFERRED MEDIUM FOR SOME OF HISTORY'S MOST FAMOUS ILLUSTRATORS INCLUDING ARTHUR RACKHAM AND E.H. SHEPARD.

Line and wash as its name implies, combines two traditional techniques, pen and ink, and watercolor. It is the method of applying flat wash tints to an ink line drawing.

BASIC EQUIPMENT It is very important to choose the correct paper for this technique. You will need a paper strong enough to resist cockling when washed, yet smooth enough to take a pen line. Smooth NOT watercolor papers fulfill these criteria, and it is worth experimenting with different types until you find the one that suits your style.

Traditional watercolor pigments and brushes are used to create the washes, while the drawing is rendered with a dip pen. Experiment with the wide range of nibs on the market to produce different widths and qualities of line. You will need to use water-proof ink, which has a tendency to dry quickly, clogging up the nib, which will need regular cleaning.

APPLICATIONS FOR THE ILLUSTRATOR Line and wash has traditionally been a popular medium for illustration, particularly of children's books, as can be seen in the books of Beatrix Potter. It is adaptable and can be used to illustrate intensely detailed work, but it can also be used very loosely.

GETTING STARTED There are three approaches to this technique; the most traditional is to start with the ink drawing. When the ink is completely dry, the color washes are then applied. The best results are achieved using thin washes. Greater intensity of color can be built up using successive layers, or by working wet-in-wet. You can, however, apply the washes first and, when they are dry, add the ink drawing afterward. The third method involves working up the two elements together, adding more line and color where necessary.

The key to success with this technique is the integration of the color with the line. Experiment with applying the washes, keeping them wet and loose, and allowing them to break out of the ink lines.

Maggie Ling
A fine example of movement and humor created by quality of line. The artist has used the dip pen with a variety of pressures to create a whole language of line.

☞
Brush Drawing; Corrections;
Enlarging and Scaling up;
Linework; Tracing and
Transferring; Watercolor.

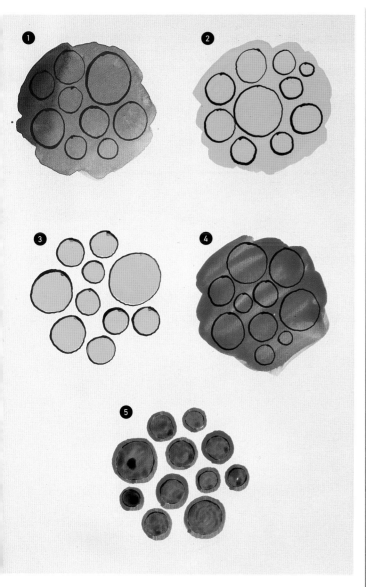

MIXING LINES AND WASHES

When choosing your line medium, it is important to bear in mind that if you wish to apply a wash on top you must use a water-resistant one.

❶ Waterproof ink and watercolor wash.
❷ Waterproof ink and gouache.
❸ Waterproof ink and gouache.
❹ Waterproof ink line and wash.
❺ Ink brush line and ink wash.

TRADITIONAL METHOD

To overcome the problem of buckling paper use pre-stretched watercolor paper, here 140lb./300gsm Hot Press, which has the smooth surface necessary for this technique. Remember to use waterproof ink, as washes are added over the line work.

1 Outline the original drawing lightly in pencil as a guide for the dip-pen line work which will be added over the top. Once dry, any visible pencil line can be removed with a kneaded (putty) eraser.

Easily obtainable, these are superior to traditional erasers as they do not leave any rubbings.

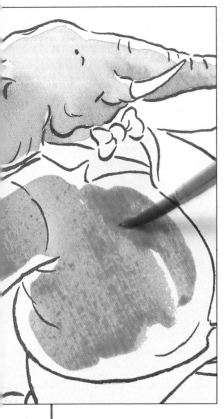

3 | Before the first wash is completely dry, add the second, darker wash. This darker wash, applied to the outside edge of his coat, will help to emphasize the elephant's rotund figure. Because the first wash is not quite dry, the two tones blend slightly, merging along the soft edge.

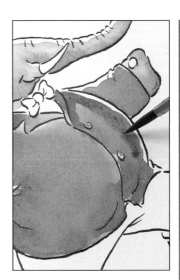

4 | This technique of two-tone washes is used to complete the whole illustration. It is important not to overwork the color, as it will lose the fresh spontaneous feel characteristic of this technique.

2 | Using the pencil lines as a guide, apply the watercolor washes with a sable brush. Two tones of each color are mixed, the palest is applied first.

Sable or synthetic brushes are suitable, but if they are to be used for brush drawing they must have a good fine point.

WASH AND LINE

An alternative for line and wash involves laying down the washes first with the linework added with a dip pen when the washes have dried. You will discover in time which technique suits you best.

1 | Outline the design with a faint pencil line. Then apply masking fluid with an old brush to the areas that are to be reserved as white paper.

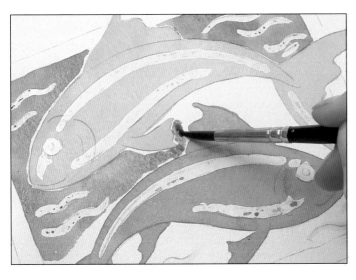

4 | A more three-dimensional quality can be added to the illustration once the linework has dried, by adding a second, darker wash, to selected areas of the design.

2 | When the masking fluid is dry (this may take a few minutes), wash over the fish and background water using a sable brush. At this stage add only the basic wash for each area. Shadow washes can be added later.

3 | Once the washes have dried, the masking fluid can be removed using a kneaded (putty) eraser, leaving the highlights on the backs of the fish, and in the water. The lines are then added with a dip pen and waterproof ink.

5 | The best quality line and wash illustration allows the illustrator to work quickly, combining individual style with a strong sense of realism.

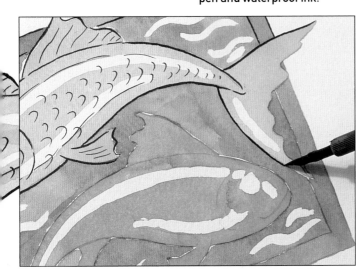

Linework

A LINE-DRAWING CAN CREATE AN ILLUSION OF DEPTH AND A SOLIDITY OF FORM, SUGGESTING A THREE-DIMENSIONAL WORLD ON A FLAT SURFACE.

As an illustrator knows, there is no such thing as a simple line. In fact, the simpler the line, the more talented the illustrator. To describe three-dimensional form with a line takes practice, but it is worth it for the illustrator because simple black and white drawings are cheap to reproduce and are much in demand.

BASIC EQUIPMENT From the earliest times, man has wished to copy the world around him, describing it with a stick in the sand or with a burnt twig on the cave wall. Today we have a vast range of media to choose from to produce a line: graphite pencils, charcoal, Conté pencils, colored pencils, brushes, felt-tip pens, crayons, oil pastels, technical pens, ballpoint pens, chalk, and dip pens, each making their own individual marks. To complement these tools, we also have a wealth of grounds to choose from, papers of different textures and weights, made from all kinds of materials including banana leaves and seaweed. This offers the opportunity to be immensely creative not only with diverse mark-making but also with color and texture.

APPLICATIONS FOR THE ILLUSTRATOR A glance through any pile of books will confirm how often linework is used by illustrators. So, for anyone who is contemplating earning a living as an illustrator, it is vitally important that they are able to draw with skill, which involves having an understanding of form. An illustrator can create his or her own individual style with an expressive line.

GETTING STARTED It is vital to experiment as much as possible with different tools for line drawing. This will enable you to become familiar with the special character of each, helping you produce your own style.

The main techniques are: outline drawing, where form is indicated with a simple outline using a single thickness of line; contour drawing, where the three-dimensional qualities of an object are outlined, for example, following the creases of a man's suit; hatching and cross-hatching, which help to create form and tone with parallel lines in close proximity, running in one, two or more different directions. With most media you can vary the thickness of the line by altering the pressure. Dip pens are particularly sensitive and create an enormous variety of line using only one nib. Other variations can be made by holding the pen or pencil in different ways and at different angles to the paper. It is also possible to work in the negative, as it were, by drawing in a white line on dark paper, or impressing. You can impress using a blunt stylus on a soft ground. The line is initially invisible, but after lightly shading over the surface, the impression remains white while the area around it takes the applied color.

Anthony Colbert
This extremely lively illustration has been created using a sketchy pen and ink line technique. The direction of the lines themselves communicates certain information, as for instance the crop in the foreground is only indicated by a series of vertical lines. The wind swept sky is described by horizontal parallel lines and cross hatching.

☞
Brush Drawing; Charcoal; Colored Pencils; Computer Illustration; Corrections; Enlarging and Scaling up; Etching; Gouache; Line and Wash; Linocut and Woodcut; Markers; Scraperboard; Tracing and Transferring.

MARK MAKING

The quality of line depends on two main factors, the medium and the paper. The following are marks made by a variety of mediums.

❶ Ballpoint pen
❷ Broad felt-tip pens
❸ Pencil
❹ Fine marker pen
❺ Medium felt-tip pen
❻ Soft pencil
❼ Conté pencil
❽ Charcoal

SILHOUETTE DRAWING

Silhouette drawing has always been a popular style for children's books. Perhaps the most famous practitioner of this style was Arthur Rackham, who used it to create detailed, magical illustrations for books like *Rip Van Winkle*. For a crisp edge to your silhouette, start by creating an outline drawing.

1 | Any drawing medium can be used with this technique, but the most traditional and expressive is the dip pen. Start by experimenting with different pressures, as this creates variations in thickness of line.

2 | Use a light pencil to outline the image, then retrace it with the dip pen. When the ink runs out, re-dip the pen. If there is too much ink in the pen, it will blot, so do a small test on a separate sheet to prevent accidents.

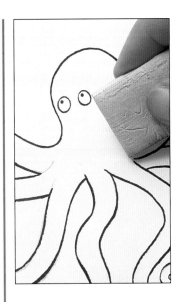

3 | When the ink is completely dry, any pencil marks showing can be erased using a kneaded eraser (putty rubber).

4 | Use a small brush and the same ink to fill in the outline to create a silhouette. Paint around the eyes of the octopus to give him character.

5 | You can speed up the drying time of the ink with a hairdryer. Be careful that it is not too hot or held too close or it may buckle the paper.

Ink and dip pens are useful for linework.

CROSSHATCHING

Crosshatching is a technique using only line work to model an area to achieve the impression of three dimensions. It is used particularly with pen and ink, but is also employed in engraving and etching.

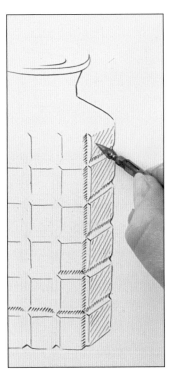

1 | This example shows how shadows can be rendered on the facets of a cut glass decanter. The first set of hatched lines are drawn in using a dip pen. Make sure that they are all parallel and the same distance apart.

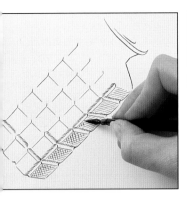

2 | For darker shadows, a second set of lines are drawn in at 90° to the original lines, forming crosshatching. This is made easier by rotating the paper. Be careful not to rest your hand on any wet ink.

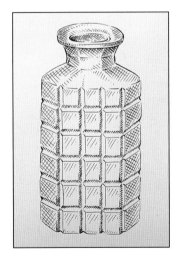

3 | To give the appearance of three dimensions, the areas of tone on each side of the decanter are built up with hatched and crosshatched lines. The closer together the lines, and the thicker they are, the darker the shadow.

CONTOUR DRAWING

With contour drawing, a subject is described by varying the outline. By making the outline thinner or thicker, rigid or soft, continuous or broken, the difference between cloth and wood is expressed. This is achieved by using the flexibility of the nib of a dip pen. A light amount of pressure with lines at a distance apart, creates lighter shading. More pressure and closer lines makes darker tones.

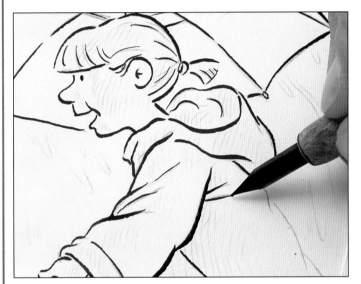

1 | The overall design is drawn lightly in pencil. It is then retraced using a dip pen, varying the line, and therefore describing the subject, by applying more or less pressure. Look closely at how the folds in the sleeves are created with a variation in thickness of the line.

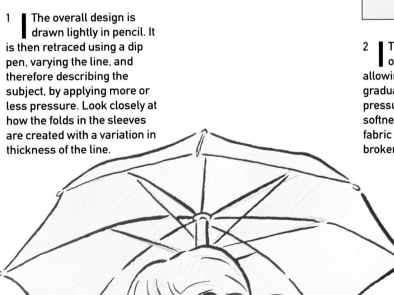

2 | The whole figure is outlined in this method, allowing the line to tail off gradually by releasing the pressure on the nib. The softness and movement of the fabric can be expressed with a broken line.

Lines do not always have to be straight; here curved lines accentuate the contour of the umbrella.

5 When the ink is thoroughly dry, any remaining pencil can be removed using a kneaded (putty) eraser. Mistakes can be removed using a scalpel or white gouache.

3 When the ink is dry, using a thinner nib and working from the top, add in shading by crosshatching. With contour drawing the lines must follow the form of the object it is describing. As the umbrella is curved, the lines are drawn to follow its contours.

6 Contour drawing is a very similar method to crosshatching, but as can be seen from the two examples, the quality of this technique is freer and more expressive.

4 From this detail it is possible to see how each individual line varies in thickness. The darker areas (the inside of the hood) are built up using thicker, closer lines.

STIPPLING

Stippling is a technique often used by the illustrator to produce soft areas of tone with dots. This method works in the same way as a black and white photograph, that is, the more densely packed the dots the darker the tone.

3 | This technique can be used with hatching and cross hatching to create a variety of textures. A ruler is used to help guide the hatching.

2 | To create the illusion of three dimensions, the spaces between the dots are varied to create lighter and darker areas, thus giving the impression of shadow and form.

4 | This technique is capable of producing extremely subtle graduations in tone. A wide range of pale gray tones can be obtained by careful control of the density of the dots, highlighted areas being left completely free of dots.

1 | This technique is suitable for both dip and technical pens. The design is first drawn out in pencil onto smooth hard paper. The image is created by following the pencil outline and applying small dots for areas of tone.

WHITE LINE

White line, or impressing, allows you to create an image using a white line against a dark background. The impressions or "white lines" can be impressed straight into the paper using a stylus or blunt paintbrush handle, "drawing" the lines into the paper. Color added over these impressed lines will leave them as white. The following technique allows you to follow an initial sketch.

1 | First, the sketch is drawn on layout paper with a light line. If the line is too dark, it will be difficult when it is retraced to see the areas you have completed.

2 Place the drawing over a piece of rough textured paper, placed on a soft surface such as layers of newspaper. Retrace the image using a pencil. Press quite hard, but be careful not to tear the paper.

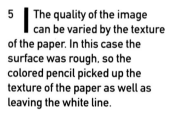

4 Next, apply the shading with a colored pencil. For a soft effect, rub the point down to create a flat section as this will give a more even tone. Try to keep the pressure even and work in the one direction only.

5 The quality of the image can be varied by the texture of the paper. In this case the surface was rough, so the colored pencil picked up the texture of the paper as well as leaving the white line.

3 Remove the layout to reveal the image impressed in the paper. If you did not press hard enough, the white lines will not appear clearly when the color is added.

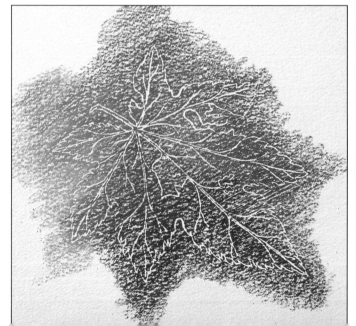

Linoleumcut and woodcut

LINOLEUMCUT AND WOODCUT ARE EXAMPLES OF RELIEF PRINTING, THE OLDEST FORM OF PRINTMAKING. WOODCUTS HAVE BEEN USED TO ILLUSTRATE BOOKS IN CHINA SINCE THE SECOND CENTURY AD, BUT IT WAS THE EXPRESSIVE POWER OF JAPANESE WOODBLOCK PRINTS WHICH SO INFLUENCED EUROPEAN ART IN THE SECOND HALF OF THE NINETEENTH CENTURY.

In relief printing, the aim is to cut away portions of the surface of the block, which can be wood, linoleum or any other suitable material, leaving the image remaining to be used as the printing surface. Ink is then applied with a roller to this surface and the impression taken.

BASIC EQUIPMENT The same type of tools can be used for both linoleum and woodcuts, although the interchangeable gouge sets sold for linoleumcut are not strong enough to be used for woodcut; use instead individual tools that have a metal shaft. It is possible, however, to start with a sturdy craft knife before investing in purpose-made tools, which makes both techniques cheap for the beginner.

The wood used for the block is sawn from along the grain, the way a plank is made. Virtually any kind of wood is suitable, from fruit woods to plywood, but you will find they handle differently and the image is affected by the wood used. The best linoleum to choose is the thick, heavy-duty kind with burlap (hessian) backing. If the linoleum is warmed before use, you will find it easier to cut into.

The most suitable paper for relief printing is thin and absorbent; traditionally, the Chinese used rice paper. Other necessary items are printing ink, a burnishing tool or spoon, and a roller.

APPLICATIONS FOR THE ILLUSTRATOR Because of their bold expressive qualities, these two techniques are suitable for illustration of all types, particularly in books, newspapers, and magazines. For limited editions, the illustration can be hand-printed. Wood blocks will last almost indefinitely, but linoleum has a limited life.

GETTING STARTED For both techniques, the composition may be drawn onto the surface of the block and the unwanted portions are then cut away, the desired image remaining as the printing surface. Always remember that the raised portion will print "black." The ink is then rolled over the surface and the paper laid on top. It is not necessary to use a printing press, the image can be printed equally well by hand-rubbing the surface with a burnishing tool such as the bowl of a spoon. The paper is then lifted by peeling it back from one corner. For color printing a separate block is used for each individual color, the impressions being printed one over the other.

LEVEL OF DIFFICULTY Linoleum is the easier of the two to begin with as it is softer to work and cheaper to make mistakes on. Once the basic skills have been mastered, you can move on to woodcut.

Lee Crocker
Traditionally linocut was printed in black only, but two or more colors can be used, presenting exciting possibilities.

☞
**Linework; Scraperboard;
Tracing and Transferring.**

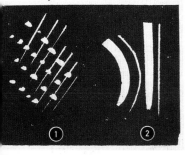

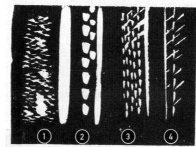

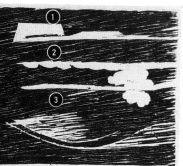

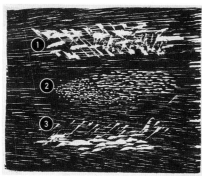

Linoleumcut

The surface of linoleum is softer and easier to work than wood, so you can work more quickly. But a linoleum block will not last as long. Producing curved lines is much easier in linoleum because there is no grain and the lines have the same clarity as those in wood. Cutting into wood feels dry and crisp, but linoleumleum has a sluggish feel. It is very important to keep your tools sharp, linoleum blunts them more quickly than wood.

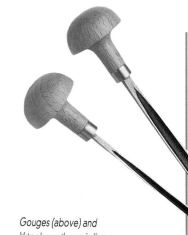

Gouges (above) and V-tools are the main lino-cutting tools.

Transferring the image

You can draw the image onto a linoleum block freehand with a soft pencil, or transfer it with traditional tracing paper. In this example yellow carbon paper is used to transfer the outline of the design from a sketch to the block.

MARK MAKING

To create different line qualities, a whole range of bought or found tools can be used, giving each mark its own unique identity.

Combining tools (top left)
V-tool and gouge
❶ The finer lines are produced with the V-tool,
❷ the thicker with the gouge.

Texture and line (top right)
❶ Rocking gouge.

❷ Gouge.
❸ V-tool.
❹ V-tool.

Textures using combined tools (bottom left)
❶ Japanese knife and gouge.
❷ Awl. On left held vertically. On right held at 45%.
❸ Japanese knife, diagonal cuts.

Line and area (bottom right)
❶ Japanese knife held at 45%.
❷ Gouge.
❸ V-tool.

Draw your design on layout paper. Attach the carbon paper to the linoleum by the top corners with tape, then anchor the sketch over the top. Trace over the outline of the image with an HB pencil.

Detailing

Having transferred the rough outline of the image with carbon paper, extra detail is then painted in with a sable brush and black India ink. This helps to give an impression of how the finished image will look once it is printed.

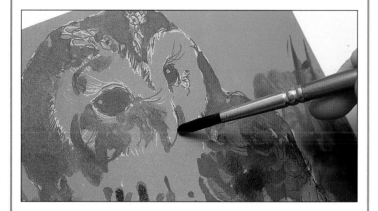

I The ink shows tonal detail rather than details of feathers, etc. The darker areas are left uncut, whereas the bare areas are textured, using a variety of different gouges to produce white lines when printed.

Sharpening

Keep your tools for linoleumcutting sharp. The most useful ones are varying sizes of "V"-shaped and rounded gouges. However, ordinary craft knives and scalpels can also be used. If these tools are not kept sharp, you may tear the soft linoleum, and blunt tools will also cause the edges of the lines to crumble.

I An oilstone is lubricated with a little light oil. The blade is then ground in a rocking motion from side to side, sharpening the cutting edge equally all over. The inside edge of the blade is sharpened with a broad slipstone, rubbed back and forth.

Gouging

With practice you will soon learn which tools create the quality of line for the desired effect. There is no specific order for cutting the design, but it is a good discipline to start with the large areas that are to print white, clearing them before you tackle the more detailed areas.

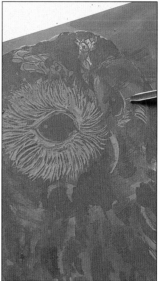

1 I When rendering animals and birds, it is the eye that really brings the creature to life, so in this example the artist had started in this area, using a fine gouge for the fine feathers spreading out from around the eye.

2 I To make the image stand out from the background of the black night sky, a larger gouge is used to create a broad outline around the form, which will print as a thick white line.

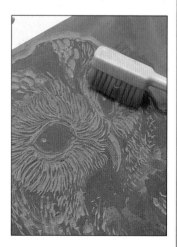

3 I When cutting, try not to gouge too deep at one time—it is easy to slip and cut into areas intended to remain untextured. An old toothbrush is useful for brushing away loose pieces of linoleum.

Inking

As with other relief printing methods, the ink is rolled out evenly, but not too thickly, with a rubber or plastic roller onto a glass slab. The ink needs to have a reasonably stiff consistency so it will not clog the finer details.

| Working methodically, roll over the design, making sure that the whole image is completely covered, picking up more ink from the slab if necessary.

Printing

With all printing processes it is essential to use the correct type of paper, i.e., one that is very thin and absorbent. The Chinese have traditionally used rice paper, which has all these qualities. To give a stronger, more velvety appearance to the print, the paper may first be dampened between sheets of wet newspaper.

1 **|** In this example a registration frame is used to place the image In the correct position on the paper. This is made from thick cardboard, placed at right angles to fit the top left-hand corner of the print. Now place the thin sheet of paper to be printed over the inked linoleumcut.

2 **|** Next, a thick sheet of paper is laid over the printing paper to protect it during burnishing. Burnishing can be done with a variety of tools; anything that has a smooth rounded end, like the back of a wooden spoon, will work.

3 **|** The final print is dramatic, with large areas of black and startling white detail and an individualistic handmade quality.

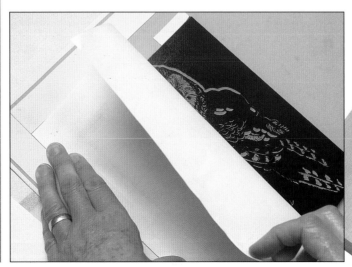

WOODCUT

Linoleumcut and woodcut are very similar processes, using the same tools and corresponding techniques. It is the different texture of each material that determines the quality of the print. As the block for woodcut is cut from the side grain, the natural pattern of the grain becomes part of the design.

Transferring the image

Unless you are particularly confident of your design, it is best to draw the image out on the wood first. This can be done with ink or pencil, or transferred with tracing or carbon paper.

The type of wood used can affect the quality of the print.

Cutting the block

The easiest direction to cut the wood is with the grain: this produces clean even lines. Running across the grain can cause the wood to splinter and produce an uneven printing surface. So it is important to practice using the tools, experimenting with different widths of gouge, to produce changes in line quality.

1 For large work, clamp your work firmly to the bench, as often it is necessary to use two hands, as in this example where a gouge and hammer are used for removing large areas.

2 A craft knife, or similar blade, can be used to cut around the outline before removing the surrounding area. This will help you produce clean edges to your line where you are running across the grain.

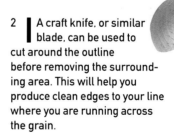

3 It is often difficult to remove tiny bits of wood from small areas after they have been cut. Working a wire brush in a circular motion will help to dislodge them.

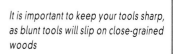

It is important to keep your tools sharp, as blunt tools will slip on close-grained woods

Applying the ink

Both hard and soft rollers are suitable for applying the ink, though a soft roller is more effective on uneven or highly textured surfaces. The ink should be of a stiff consistency: if it is too thin, it will flood the finer lines and spoil the print.

Printing

As with all forms of relief printing, it is important to use an absorbent thin paper. This can be used dry, or to produce an even denser, more velvety quality, it can be dampened between layers of damp newspaper.

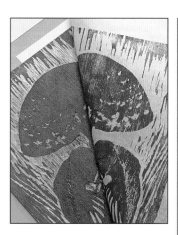

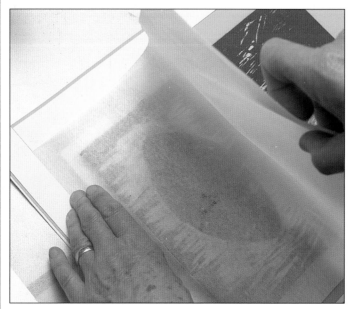

1 The paper is laid carefully over the block. Make sure it does not move on the wood, as this will cause a blurred image.

After the ink has been rolled onto a glass inking plate, the roller is passed over the surface of the block twice, once away from you, then toward you.
Make sure not to over-ink the surface, as this will produce a smudged print.

2 A clean sheet of thicker paper is then placed over the top. The image is then burnished onto the paper. You can use any round-ended instrument such as the back of a wooden spoon.

3 Remove the cover paper. The print can then be detached, peeling it off by one corner slowly to prevent tearing the paper.

4 The image produced is much bolder and more expressive than can be achieved in wood engraving, and differs from linoleumcut in that it takes on the qualities of the wood.

Markers

WIDELY USED FOR VISUALIZATION, MARKER PENS HAVE A SPONTANEITY AND DIRECTNESS OF APPLICATION THAT CAN PRODUCE A WIDE RANGE OF EFFECTS.

Markers use a similar technique to watercolor, where the intensity of tone and color is built up in layers, leaving the paper white for the lightest areas. The colors are overlaid as with watercolor washes to darken tones and mix colors.

BASIC EQUIPMENT There are two main types of marker pen, solvent-based and water-soluble. They come with all sorts of tip sizes and shapes for producing a wide variety of lines. Don't be tempted to buy pens in boxed sets as you will probably buy more than you need. Always test the marker in the shop as it is difficult to know how long it has been sitting on the shelf, and make sure that the color on the lid matches the actual color of the pen.

Solvent markers can be toxic, so work in a well-ventilated room. To help prolong the life of your markers, make sure the tops are on properly. If a solvent-based marker shows signs of running out, a few drops of rubber-cement thinner applied to the felt core inside the marker can help it last twice as long.

A type of paper is made specifically for this medium; surprisingly enough, it is usually called marker paper. Layout paper, however, works equally well, but use a sheet of card between layers to prevent bleeding.

APPLICATIONS FOR THE ILLUSTRATOR Markers are most suitable for layouts, concept ideas, story boards, fashion, and architectural illustrations. It has become the standard layout medium for design studios and advertising agencies. Computer graphics have not replaced this form of visualization although the two are usually used in tandem, with the visual scanned in to be manipulated by the computer.

GETTING STARTED Many people have used felt-tipped pens of some sort since infancy and are not intimidated by them. The strength of this medium is its freshness and spontaneity; they therefore need to be used with confidence.

Marker pads come with a waxed paper sheet, which is used to prevent the marker from bleeding through onto the sheets beneath, so make sure you place it under the page you are working on. Before you start, try to have a strong image in mind as markers are indelible and difficult to correct.

There are two accepted basic styles of marker visual. The first is primarily used for quick layouts, where the marker strokes are visible. The second is for finished visuals, where the strokes are blended into flat areas of color to give a highly polished finish.

The main aim when using markers is to try to capture strong light and shade, modeling form with simplified tones. When covering an area with either color or tone, use strong directional strokes that overlap slightly to create an area of flat tone and prevent white gaps. A paper mask can be used for crisp edges. Various textured effects can be obtained by using partly dried-out markers. Because marker paper is thin, lighter tones can be achieved by working on the reverse of the paper.

☞

Charcoal; Collage and Mixed Media; Colored Pencils; Corrections; Enlarging and Scaling up; Line and Wash; Linework; Masking Techniques; Tracing and Transferring; Watercolor.

Andrew Fowlkes
Marker pens are used extensively as a visualizing medium. This image was created as a visual for product development, to help the client imagine the finished look of the product.

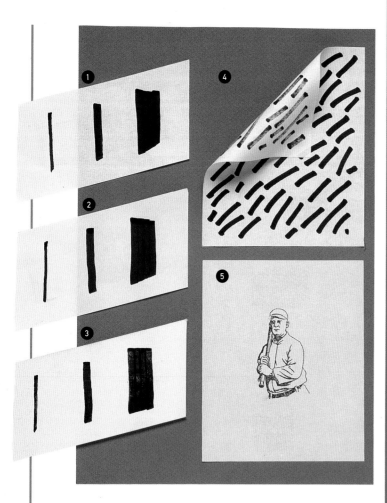

BLENDING COLORS

The main consideration when using markers is to use them as confidently as possible. Often beginners will use short scratchy strokes, leaving small white patches of paper showing through, thus making the image appear fragmented. It is vital for finished visuals, that the image appears as solid as possible.

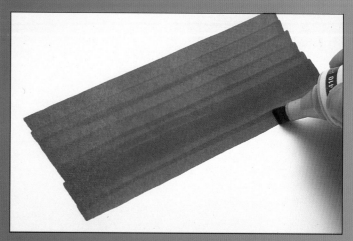

1 Blending colors successfully is achieved by applying the color in overlapping parallel lines, in this case the darker color is applied first.

2 In the same way, the second color is laid down. Apply the color at a consistent speed or the tone will vary.

DIFFERENT NIBS

Marker pens can be bought in a variety of nib thicknesses. In these examples a thin, medium and thick marker has been applied to various types of paper.
1 Layout paper.
2 Bleedproof marker paper.
3 CS 10 paper.

4 Layout paper, paler tone on reverse side of paper.
5 Dry transfer. An image can be taken from a black and white photocopy by rubbing the reverse with a marker pen.

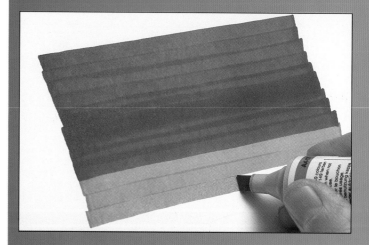

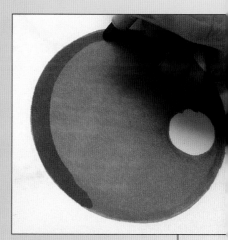

CREATING FORM

When trying to give the impression of three-dimensional form on a two-dimensional flat surface, the most important consideration is the direction of the light, and therefore the areas of shadow. It may be helpful to set up a small still life, similar to your subject, and experiment with lighting it at different angles.

3 | Now give the top two thirds of the darker area a second coat, leaving a mid tone area near the join.

4 | This mid-tone area is then blended with the lighter area by laying parallel lines of the lighter blue over the top. This color is then continued down over the lighter area, thus blending the two together.

1 | In this example a simple sphere is colored, with the strokes going in the same direction, leaving a circular highlight. Smaller highlights can be added later with gouache or white pencil.

2 | Next add a second coat of the same color with strokes in the opposite direction so that the color is flat and consistent. A darker tone of blue is added along the edge opposite the highlight.

3 | These two tones of blue are then blended by superimposing more layers of the lighter tone. This graduates the color from the darker shadow side, toward the highlight.

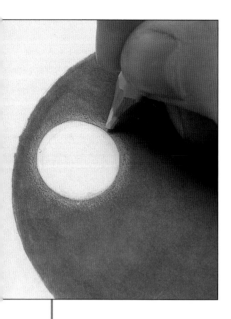

4 The edge of the highlight is hard and looks a little unrealistic, this can be softened and tidied up by applying white pencil to the very edge of the color. As white pencil leaves small areas of the base color showing through, it gives the impression of a lighter tone.

TIDYING

It is easy to stray over the outline but such mistakes are also easily rectified. This can be done by either removing or covering the mistake.

If the paper is strong enough, gently scrape away the unwanted marks with a sharp scalpel blade. Alternatively, paint white gouache over the offending area, as shown here.

CREATING AN OBJECT

Marker visuals use a combination of the techniques previously described. Success is determined by the speed and confidence of the application of the color, and an understanding of the form. It relies on the strong use of light and shade, so try to use two contrasting tones for each color.

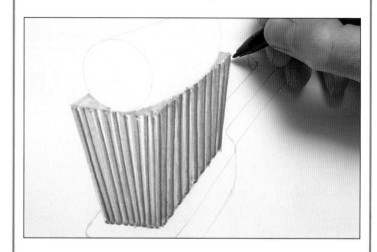

1 The design is first drawn in pencil. Keeping in mind the position of the highlights, add the lightest tones first. Details can be added with finer fiber tipped pens.

2 Darker tones can be added either with a darker marker or by applying another layer of the same color. Subtle changes of tone can be built up with successive layers of the same color.

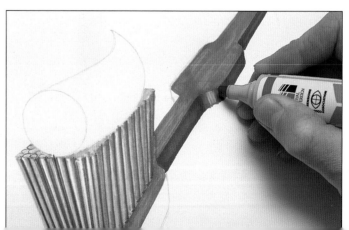

3 | Work on the whole image. Do not complete individual areas and then move onto another, as the overall solidity of the form can be lost. Build up detail gradually all over.

4 | Although you may have left highlighted areas as white paper, make them really crisp and give the visual a slick appearance with white gouache. For straight lines use a ruler to help guide the brush.

LETRAJET

If all the equipment and expense necessary for airbrush work seems beyond your reach, a simpler and cheaper alternative is the small spray attachment for a marker pen. It uses the same principle of compressed air to disperse color evenly onto a surface, but it uses canned air and marker ink. Of course it is not so versatile as an airbrush but can save you time and be useful for filling in flat or graduated areas of color.

1 | The marker spray attachment is useful for providing graduated backgrounds for marker visuals. Masking can be used to give the work a clean crisp edge or for protecting a completed image. Make sure you use a sharp blade when cutting the mask.

2 | Using short bursts of air, with the spray held at a distance from the paper, pass the spray in parallel lines over the surface. To create a graduated effect, repeat the process, covering all but the bottom section of the page and spray each successive layer covering slightly less.

3 | If the mask is not stuck tightly to the paper, the pigment will creep underneath. For a really crisp edge, masking film is most reliable or alternatively low-tack masking or magic tape.

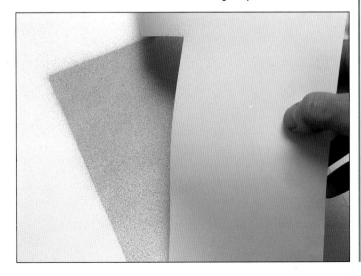

Masking techniques

THE ILLUSTRATOR, ALWAYS SHORT OF TIME, IS CONSTANTLY ON THE LOOKOUT FOR WAYS OF SPEEDING UP REPETITIVE ACTIONS. STENCILS, TEMPLATES AND MASKS CAN ALL HELP THE BUSY ILLUSTRATOR.

Stencils, templates and masks are used for simple print-making, creating a guide to aid the drawing of repeated or complex shapes, and for masking off an area of the paper or ground. All involve the cutting of a guide, from paper, cardboard or plastic.

BASIC EQUIPMENT Stencils can be cut with a craft knife from paper, cardboard, thin plastic sheet, or special screen-printing paper. There are specialist brushes on the market that have densely packed, very short bristles which are designed for stencilling. Gouache and acrylic paints are particularly suitable for stencilling because the paint has some body and dries quickly.

Templates are usually cut from thicker materials than stencils, as they are used as a guide for the drawing implement. Thick cardboard or even wood or metal can be used.

Masks can be made from almost anything from paper to household objects. Masking tape is ideal for creating sharp straight lines, frisk film is used in conjunction with an air-brush, and masking fluid is used for smaller areas and is suitable for water-based mediums.

APPLICATIONS FOR THE ILLUSTRATOR Stencils are useful for repeating simple images. They can be used for borders, for posters or within the illustration process. Perhaps the best-known templates are set squares, ellipse guides and French curves, which can be bought ready cut. However it is possible to cut your own to save time on repetitive measurements. Masking can be used to give a sharp clean edge to an illustration, protect isolated areas, or to create effects within the image itself.

GETTING STARTED When you cut a stencil, you have to think negatively, cutting away the areas which form the image that will appear on the paper. Once the stencil is completed, it is then placed on the ground. The tip of the brush is dipped in the paint and the excess wiped off. The paint should not be too dilute or it will seep under the stencil. Hold the brush vertically, apply to the exposed ground, and build up the color by repeating the process. A more tricky, but effective, method is to apply acrylic paint direct from the tube onto the edge of the stencil and then scrape it across the cut-out sections with a spatula. The stencil then has to be lifted carefully by one corner, leaving the image embossed in thick paint on the ground.

Templates are often used as a precision instrument in mechanical drawings so they need to be accurately cut or bought ready-made. Any drawing instrument can be used to draw around the template, but if you are using ink, make sure that it does not seep under the guide.

Examples of masking can be seen on the walls of caves, paintings dating back tens of thousands of years. The simplest method of masking is to spray paint onto a surface using your hand as the mask. To create a sharp edge, masking tape is placed in the desired place; the edges are firmly rubbed down, then paint is applied overlapping the tape. When it is dry peel the tape off carefully. Note this method is not suitable for light smooth papers. Masking fluid is slightly colored to help detection when dry. Apply it with an old brush as it will ruin a good one. Once dry, the paint can be applied over the top and it will reserve the white paper underneath. Wet washes will produce the best effects. Once the paint is dry, the masking fluid can be removed by rubbing with your finger or an eraser, revealing the white paper underneath.

☞

Acrylic; Airbrushing; Collage and Mixed Media; Colored Pencils; Gouache; Markers; Pastels; Resist Techniques; Watercolor.

MAKING A PAPER MASK

This is probably the easiest form of mask making, and can be used to create simple or even quite complex forms, though to prevent damage to finer work it is necessary to use thicker card. When applying paint media, make sure they are not too dilute or they will bleed under the mask.

2 In this example a thin wash of acrylic paint has been applied to the background. The mask is then held In place while oil pastel is applied around the masked area.

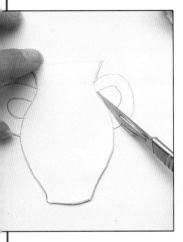

1 Any type of heavy card or paper is suitable for this technique. The outline is drawn in pencil and then cut out with a new scalpel blade or craft knife.

3 Make sure that you have applied pastel up to the very edge of the mask. On a larger area, this process can be used over and over to produce a repeat pattern.

MASKING TAPE

Masking tape can be used for crisp edges around your illustration. When using fine Hot Press papers, take care when removing the tape or you may damage the paper.

1 Before the masking tape is applied, measure the dimensions of your illustration using a set square, and pencil in lightly. Now carefully lay down the masking tape only pressing down the inside edge, taking particular care at the corners. Next apply the wash as usual.

2 Make sure that the wash is completely dry before removing the tape. Each strip is lifted off separately and slowly. taking care not to tear the paper.

3 The result is clean and crisp. If the paint has seeped under the tape, scratch it out with a scalpel.

MASKING FILM

This technique is normally associated with airbrushing, but it can be equally effective with other waterbased media. It is particularly useful if you wish to leave a large area white when using a broad medium for the background, such as spattering, or as in this case, a very wet watercolor wash.

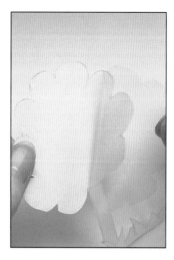

2 The backing is then peeled off carefully to prevent the film from tearing. Start at one corner and pull slowly and evenly, particularly in the detailed areas.

1 Masking film comes attached to a paper backing onto which you can draw your design. Then, using a new blade in a craft knife or scalpel, cut around the edge of the image.

3 This technique works best with smoother papers and will need very little pressing down. It can be used with more textured papers, but it will need pressure to attach it firmly.

4 The paint is then applied with a large brush. Try not to scrub too vigorously around the edges. To prevent the film from lifting, drag the brush from the center to right and left.

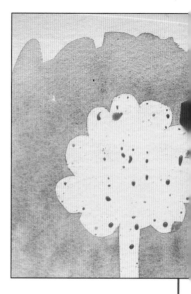

5 It is important to leave the design until the paint is absolutely dry before removing the film. You may need to lift the edge with the point of a scalpel first, as it can be a little tricky to pick up.

MASKING FLUID

Masking fluid, or frisket, is an extremely successful technique for masking small detailed areas and fine lines. It is made from a clear rubber latex solution, but it can be bought with a yellow tint for use on white paper, thus allowing you to see where it has been applied.

1 | The design is sketched lightly in pencil before the fluid is applied with a brush. Masking fluid can be difficult to remove from the bristles, so use an old brush.

2 | Make sure the fluid is completely dry before applying any paint. This technique can be used with any waterbased pigment and, as in this example, is extremely successful with watercolor.

3 | Once the paint has dried, remove the masking fluid with a clean finger or an eraser (rubber). Any pencil marks under the fluid will be removed, leaving a clean white area.

4 | Masking fluid can be used at any stage and can be applied over a dry wash to protect it from the next, allowing you to build up color while leaving small areas of the original base color.

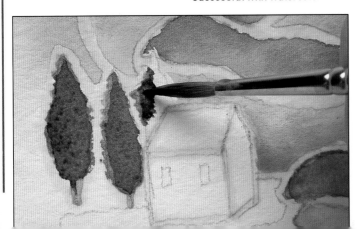

STENCILS – MOP BRUSH

This technique has become extremely fashionable in interior design, but can also be used very effectively in illustration work, used, for instance, to reproduce a repeat border design. Few specialist materials are required, and both the special stencil paper and the mop brushes are widely available and relatively inexpensive.

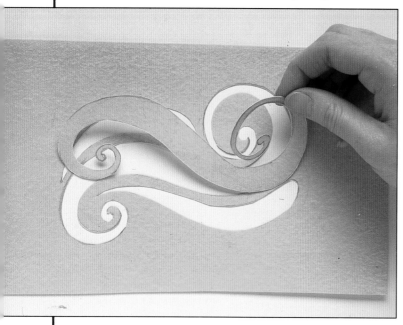

2 | It is very important to work out your design carefully. Make it as simple as possible. Cutting out small detailed areas can be a little tricky.

3 | Tape the stencil firmly to the drawing paper; any weight or type of surface is suitable. Any waterbased pigment can be used, but keep the mop brush very dry and dab it onto the paper using a light repetitive motion.

4 | In this example three colors were used one on top of the other, leaving each layer to dry before applying the next. It is advisable to wash off previous colors before re-using the stencil.

1 | Stencil paper is fairly stiff and has a smooth waxed surface that can be wiped clean and reused many times. The design is drawn in pencil on the stencil paper and then cut out with a sharp knife.

USING A SPATULA

With the mop brush technique, the painted area is made up of very small dots of color, so the effect is soft and almost mossy. To achieve a stronger, bolder effect, try the spatula technique.

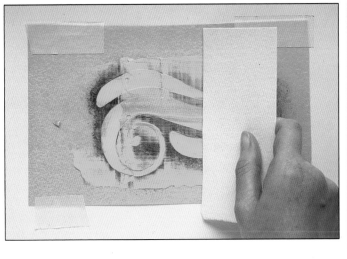

3 | Repeat this process if you miss small areas.

4 | Before removing the stencil, let the paint dry a little to prevent smudging. If you use too much pigment, the paint can bleed under the stencil, so experimenting with the consistency and amount of paint before you create the final image may be helpful.

1 | The stencil is prepared in exactly the same way as for the mop brush and attached to the drawing paper. Then a blob of paint is applied at one end of the stencil.

2 | With a piece of stiff cardboard, pull the paint over the design, pressing firmly and moving the spatula slowly and evenly.

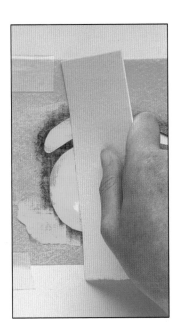

Monoprint

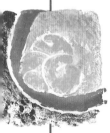

TO MAKE A MONOPRINT, YOU WILL NEED ONLY THE SIMPLEST STUDIO EQUIPMENT AND, UNLIKE SOME OTHER PRINTING PROCESSES, THIS TECHNIQUE NEEDS NO PRESS, MAKING IT A GOOD ONE FOR BEGINNERS.

The process allows you, the artist, to produce either a single or a limited number of reproductions. A monoprint differs from painting directly onto paper because there is a unique quality of texture produced by the pressure of printing. Having mastered the basic principles, there are few standard methods, allowing the artist a great amount of freedom. Accidental effects are encouraged, making it an exciting medium to work in.

BASIC EQUIPMENT The image is painted in any medium that does not dry rapidly—ordinary oil paint, printing inks or even some water-based paints—onto any flat, smooth and non-absorbent material, such as glass, metal or plastic. This can be done with anything that can make a mark: brushes, palette knives, sponges or rollers. The completed image is then transferred onto paper by laying the paper on the painted surface and pressing the back with a roller, spoon or even your hand. Different textures of paper can extend the range of effects.

Theresa Pateman
The technique of monoprint enables the artist to create unexpected random textures that can add a new dimension to a piece of work.

APPLICATIONS FOR THE ILLUSTRATOR As an illustration technique, the monoprint method can be extremely effective, producing in a short time an image that, because it cannot be too detailed, reproduces well.

GETTING STARTED Monoprinting is a basic technique that can be mastered quickly, enabling the artist to produce a professional result in a short time.

You will find it easiest to start with a sheet of glass as your painting surface. Use your own sketch as a guide, placing it underneath the glass. Apply your ink or paint to the surface of the glass, as if you were painting on paper, following your sketch. When your image is complete, lay a sheet of relatively absorbent paper on the glass and press firmly and evenly on the back. When the paper is peeled off, you will have the reverse of your original image.

There are many ways you can experiment further, for example, with glazes of color built up on the original print, or with linework added before taking a second impression.

PAPER TEXTURES
As with many other techniques the choice of paper will affect how your finished monoprint will look.
❶ Hot-pressed papers will pick up the texture from the paint and will not influence the result with any texture of its own.
❷ Not paper will give a medium texture.
❸ Rough paper is so highly textured that it may pick up very little pigment.

Acrylic; Brush Drawing; Gouache.

MONOPRINTING ON GLASS

It is important to make sure that you have all the necessary equipment before you start. You need a clean sheet of glass (cover the edges with tape), layout paper, watercolor paper, a small roller, and printing inks. Give yourself plenty of room and keep the working area clear.

1 | A rough sketch is designed and colored onto a sheet of layout paper and placed under the piece of glass. To make sure that the registration does not alter, make pencil marks on the edge of the glass and transfer them to the sketch paper.

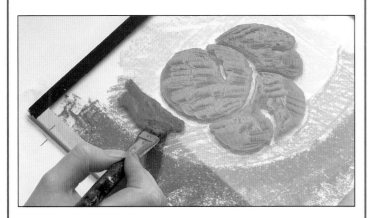

2 | Using the sketch as a pattern, the printing inks are then painted onto the glass with a chisel brush. In this case, a white edge is left around each of the objects to enhance the impression of a printed image.

3 | The printing paper is then laid over the glass and rubbed firmly with your fist or a small printing roller. Do not allow the paper to slide on the plate, or the image will smudge.

4 | The paper can then be carefully peeled off the plate: hold down one corner and gradually lift it off. If there is still ink on the plate, a second impression can be taken, though it will be paler than the first.

Pastels

FOR BOLD AND EXPRESSIVE WORK, PASTELS ARE AN IDEAL MEDIUM. THEY CAN PRODUCE STRONG SATURATED COLORS OR DELICATE AREAS OF TEXTURED LINEWORK, ALLOWING THE ILLUSTRATOR THE OPPORTUNITY TO PRODUCE INTENSE IMAGES.

There are two main types of pastels, oil and chalk. They use similar techniques, but oil pastel can be used with turpentine or white spirit, as a solvent.

BASIC EQUIPMENT Oil and chalk pastels vary not only in their ingredients, but also in their textures. Oils are waxy and produce a bolder mark, chalks are softer altogether. They can be used on a range of paper textures, but special pastel paper comes in a range of tints with a rough and smooth side. Oil pastels can be used on fine-grade sandpaper but remember not to blend colors with your finger.

There are three types of chalk pastel. First, soft pastels which have a high proportion of pigment to binder, this gives them a rich texture and very brilliant colors. However, they have a tendency to snap and because of their powdery texture can be slightly uncontrollable. Second, hard pastels which are stronger because they contain more binder. Third, pastel pencils are encased in wood, which makes

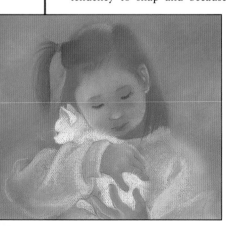

Nagako Suzuki
The finished effect of a chalk pastel illustration is strongly influenced by the paper used. For this piece, the artist has used one of the standard pastel papers, and small dots of the underlying texture can be seen through the pigment.

them cleaner and easier to use but gives different results. Pastels are renowned for being rather messy to work with, so it is as well to prepare the work area with this in mind. For chalk pastels a strong fixative is recommended.

APPLICATIONS FOR THE ILLUSTRATOR Pastel lends itself particularly to bold, dramatic subjects, and can create strong mood, it is least suited to detailed work.

GETTING STARTED Oil pastels can be blended by "feathering" where long and short parallel lines weave the colors into each other, or by working one color into another. The base color can be revealed later by scratching the top color away. Turpentine can be added to pastel work with a brush to combine paint techniques with those of the pastel stick.

Chalk pastels are applied in much the same manner. Colors can be mixed or blended with your finger, brush, or a torchon or by optical mixing. Variations can be introduced with accents of color and areas of stippling. Hard pastel is mainly used for sketching. The medium has been popular throughout the history of art for monochromatic drawing. The technique uses colored paper to produce the middle tones, white for the highlights and lighter shades, and black or sepia for the darkest areas.

PASTEL LINE STROKES
Pastels can be used to build up an entire picture using a network of lines, known as hatching.

❶ Hot-pressed paper with: oil pastel; chalk pastel.
❷ Cold-pressed paper with: oil pastel; chalk pastel.
❸ Rough paper with: oil pastel; chalk pastel.

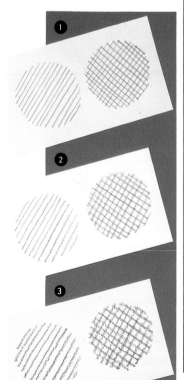

☞
Charcoal; Collage and Mixed Media; Colored Pencils; Corrections; Linework; Masking Techniques.

OIL PASTEL: BURNISHING AND SCRATCHING BACK

Oil pastel, like chalk pastel, can be applied in a multitude of ways, very softly, allowing the paper to show through, or with more pressure, which deposits more pigment. Colors can be superimposed one on another and then blended with a finger or torchon, or by "feathering" the colors one into another, using interlinking strokes. Oil pastels differ from chalk pastels in texture. They are not chalky, more waxy. This means they can be built up in thick layers and burnished and scratched into to introduce a linear dimension. Oil pastels can also be blended and manipulated with a solvent.

2 | Once the color has been built up and burnished, linear detail can be added by scratching into the pigment with a blunt stylus or the end of a paint brush, revealing the paler ground underneath.

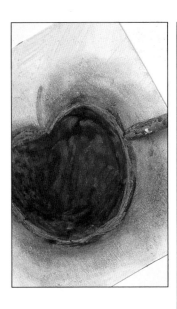

PASTEL BLENDING EFFECTS

The results achievable with pastel vary dramatically depending on the type of paper used. With smooth papers the pastel covers the whole surface evenly; with rougher papers, the pastel only adheres to the raised areas therefore less pigment is laid down on the surface.

❶ Hot-pressed paper with: oil pastel; chalk pastel.
❷ Cold-pressed paper with: oil pastel; chalk pastel.
❸ Rough paper with: oil pastel; chalk pastel.

1 | In this example, layers of pigment are applied, building up an intense and saturated area of color. To enhance the color, a burnishing tool or, alternatively, a fingernail can be gently rubbed over the oil pastel in this area.

3 | The outline, as well as the contours of the apple described with hatched lines, are scratched into the pastel.

OIL PASTEL: REVEAL
As an illustration technique, reveal can be extremely effective. You may find that warming the pastels gently before use will help soften them. This will help you to build up the amount of pigment on the paper necessary for this technique.

2 | The underlayer is then covered with darker layers of pigment, until the pale layer is completely covered. You will have to keep tearing off the cover paper from the pastel, as this will scratch off the pigment.

1 | Starting with pale colors, build up an underlayer of mixed tones. Rough paper is particularly suitable as it helps you to apply a thicker layer of pastel and catches the underlayer in its depressions so that it, and not the paper, is revealed.

There are many varieties of pastel on the market and they all look rather similar, so be sure to read the labels to check which you are buying. oil pastel (right); wax pastel (opposite).

3 | With a blunt point such as the end of a paintbrush, the design can then be scratched into the surface revealing the underlayer. The thickness of line depends on the tool you use.

OIL PASTEL: USING SOLVENTS

Although oil pastels have a thick, waxy texture, they can be worked into with a solvent to produce thin transparent washes. Oil pastels are soluble in turpentine or mineral spirits (white spirit). A variety of techniques can be used. The paper can be soaked first in turpentine or oil and then drawn on or, as in this example, the pastel drawing can be worked into with the solvent.

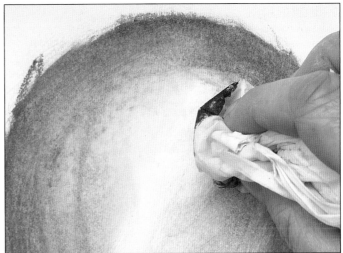

2 | The turpentine or mineral spirits (white spirit) is applied to a clean tissue or piece of kitchen paper towel, which is then used to blend and spread the color over the image with small circular strokes.

3 | Allow the solvent to dry, and then add more pastel over the top. If the paper remains wet, the overlaid pastel will bleed, making the line fuzzy. You can deliberately exploit this property to produce interesting results.

1 | This technique works particularly well with rougher papers. The outline is sketched in using a mix of colors laid down in thick strokes.

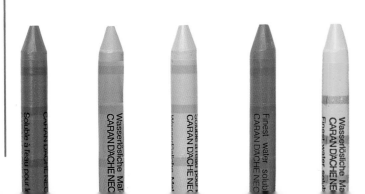

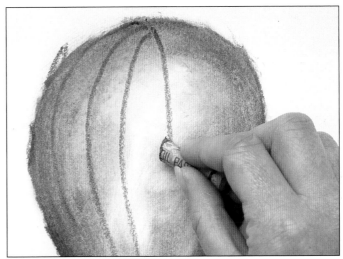

4 | Further blending can be done with a finger and the solvent-soaked paper towel, gradually building up the image. For small detailed areas, a cotton swab (bud) can be soaked in turpentine and used.

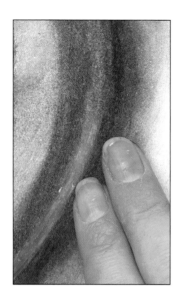

5 | This technique can be used to produce a variety of effects, including rendering distance, perspective, and atmospheric conditions such as mist and smoke haze.

BLENDING CHALK PASTEL

Because of the lovely soft nature of chalk pastel, it is an ideal medium for decorative, impressionistic illustrations, created with blending techniques. A wide variety of papers are suitable as a background, including highly textured and colored ones. When the work is completed, it is vital to use a fixative to prevent unwanted smudging. This has the effect of bonding the pastel to the paper.

1 | Over a creamy-yellow textured pastel paper, apply the background yellow with a small length of chalk used horizontally. Now blend the pastel surface gently with the pads of your fingers. Blow off any excess chalk.

2 | Darker colors are then applied over the background. Note how the texture of the paper breaks up the pastel strokes to create optical blending.

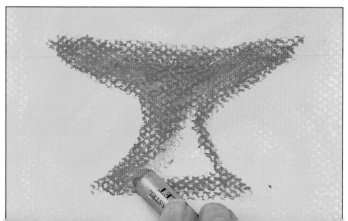

There are many makes of chalk pastel on the market from the traditional circular stick (below), to the square variety (right). Both come in a whole rainbow of colors.

3 | This time your blending finger both softens the pastel strokes and blends the colors together. Pastel work is messy, but you could blend with a paper stump or torchon.

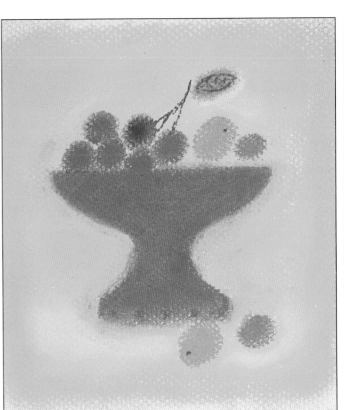

4 | As more detail is added, it can be seen how the texture of the paper enhances the qualities of the chalk pastel to soften the image even more.

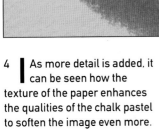

5 | Colors can be blended into one another to produce a wide variety of tones. Here the background color has been strengthened around the edge, with paler yellow added around the image, to create a soft frame.

Resist techniques

WITH MEMORIES OF CHILDHOOD FUN, THIS TECHNIQUE EXPLOITS THE FACT THAT WAXY SUBSTANCES REPEL WATER, OFFERING THE ILLUSTRATOR THE OPPORTUNITY FOR NUMEROUS HAPPY ACCIDENTS.

With resist techniques, you work from light to dark, covering areas or drawing with wax crayon or candle to reserve the white paper beneath. Wash over with a water-based paint and repeat the process if required.

BASIC EQUIPMENT For the resist, you can use any medium that contains oil or wax, from wax crayons, to pastels or candles. However it is worth experimenting a little to find those that most efficiently repel water. With rough paper, it is possible to produce a wide range of textures. Make sure that, if you are using a lot of wet washes, the paper is of a heavy weight so that it does not cockle. Any water-based paint is suitable, from watercolors to acrylics and inks.

APPLICATIONS FOR THE ILLUSTRATOR Resist techniques are useful for introducing an interesting area of texture into a piece of artwork, such as a patch of white water in a watercolor, or you can use the technique to produce a unique style of your own for any branch of illustration. The results are often bold so they reproduce well.

GETTING STARTED To achieve the best results in this medium, it has to be used decisively. Do not attempt too much detail, and try to work as freely as possible.

You can start by producing swatches of different patterns using the resist method with a pale-colored wax crayon and a dark wash of watercolor. When you are ready to tackle a whole work, try using a white candle and watercolors. Study your subject carefully before you begin, mapping out with a pencil the lightest areas, those in the middle tone, and those in shadow. Once the wax is applied, it is difficult to remove. You must work in a systematic manner, starting with the highlights, which are reserved in wax first. An overall wash is then painted over the whole area, making sure it is not too dark. Once this wash has dried, wax in the mid-tone areas and apply another slightly darker wash. You can repeat this process again and again, layering on darker and darker washes, applying the wax between each, to preserve the color of the previous wash.

This technique may also be tried with oil pastels in the place of wax. This offers the opportunity to bring in extra color and texture.

Anthony Colbert
This gouache resist illustration shows the effectiveness of a strong quality of line. Each individual mark has a direction and shape, some being almost wedge shaped. The illustrator has used the style of linoleumcut to influence his image.

> ☞
> Acrylic; Collage and Mixed Media; Etching; Gouache; Ink; Pastels; Watercolor.

ACRYLIC AND OIL PASTEL

This technique is not wildly different from a method many of us will have tried in school, but instead of poster paint, which has a tendency to be lumpy, acrylic pigments are used with oil pastel.

OIL PAINT AND ACRYLIC

This method works on the same principle as oil pastel and acrylic, but because oil paint has a greater covering ability and gives more varied textural effects, this technique allows a wider variety of effects.

1 Draw the basic outline in pencil if necessary, and then trace it in oil pastel. Keep in mind that the areas covered with oil pastel will not be colored by the acrylic.

2 This technique is most effective if the paint is a thin consistency, since the oil can resist the waterbased paint more effectively. White oil pastel is used for areas such as highlight.

The oil paint is applied first and allowed to dry completely before acrylic is painted over it. Make sure you use a wet wash of acrylic to maximize the resist effect.

Scraperboard

BY SCRAPING INTO A BLACK-COATED BOARD WITH A SHARP POINT, DRAMATIC BLACK AND WHITE IMAGES CAN BE CREATED.

Sharp tools of different shapes are used to scratch away the black surface of the specially-coated or previously inked board, revealing the white clay primer underneath. Techniques developed for relief printing (see Etching and Linocut and Woodcut) are effective for scraperboard.

BASIC EQUIPMENT There are three main scraping heads used for this technique which can be fitted into a pen nib holder: lozenge-shaped cutters, gouges, and knife blades. Each is used to create different marks, some for fine lines, others for larger areas.

Two types of scraperboard are available. One has a white clay surface which is inked over before use, the other comes with a black coating of ink. You will also need a bottle of waterproof drawing ink and a soft, flat brush.

Graham Berry
The artist has used watercolor washes over a black and white scraperboard illustration.

APPLICATIONS FOR THE ILLUSTRATOR Scraperboard was very popular in the first half of this century and is still a widely used medium for illustration, being particularly suitable for the monochrome reproduction used in newspapers and magazines, and being cheap to produce.

GETTING STARTED This technique needs to be worked decisively, so it is necessary to work out your composition ca·efully before you start, to reduce the risk of error. You can correct mistakes, however, by inking them over, which works well on artwork for reproduction.

If you have started with a white surface, the first step is to ink over the areas necessary for the design, using a soft, flat brush and applying a thin even coat. Once the board is thoroughly dry, follow your design and first establish any large black or white areas, then add the mid-tones using hatching and cross-hatched strokes or areas of stippling. Scraperboard tools provide the means of achieving a wide variety of marks, but any sharp point can be used.

The style that gives the simplest, most effective image using this technique is pure linework, fine white lines etched out of the black background. But it is also the most difficult to achieve, as there is little margin for error. Other useful techniques include parallel line cuts, silhouette, line and cross-hatched tone, and a broad woodcut style.

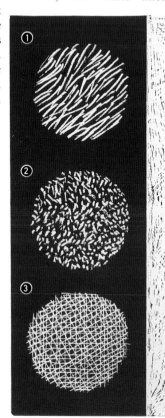

MARK MAKING
Creating a variety of line effects with different tools will give your work vibrancy and expression
❶ Marks made by a lozenge tool.
❷ Marks made with a gouge.
❸ Crosshatching produced with a knife.

☞
Etching: Linocut and Woodcut; Tracing and Transferring; Wood Engraving.

Scraperboard nibs are divided into four basic shapes (from left): lozenge shape gives medium to broad lines; another lozenge shape gives medium to fine lines; knife blade type is good for clearing large areas and broad single shapes; gouge shape gives medium lines, small dots and circles when used to lightly drill the surface.

PUTTING IN NIBS

As well as using scraperboard nibs, you can also obtain a whole variety of line effects with less conventional tools such as pins, scalpels, or even butter-curlers as well as traditional engraving tools. It is most important to keep your tools sharp, as a blunt tool slows down your work dramatically.

As scraperboard nibs can be very sharp, take care when pushing them into the handle.

TRANSFERRING THE IMAGE

If you are feeling confident, your design can be drawn onto the board either with white chalk or white pencil. Perhaps a safer technique is to transfer the image by tracing it from a rough sketch, which allows you to develop the design fully.

1 The design is first drawn in pencil onto tracing paper. Then, on the reverse side, the image is covered with white chalk or pastel.

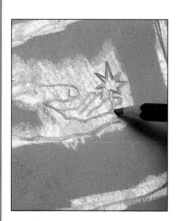

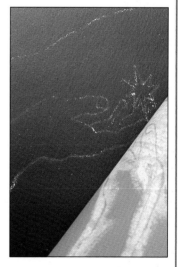

2 The tracing paper is then laid over the scraperboard, chalk side down, and taped at the edges to prevent movement. Using a pencil or stylus, the design is then drawn over.

3 It is advisable to keep checking to see how well the image is showing up, as you may need to adjust the pressure to transfer the image successfully. Make sure the tracing paper does not slip.

HATCHING AND CROSSHATCHING

This technique produces the illusion of different tones, using a series of parallel lines at differing widths and distances from one another. With finer lines hatched widely apart, there will be more black printed, so the eye reads the areas as a dark tone. The thicker the line and narrower the distance between them, the lighter the tone.

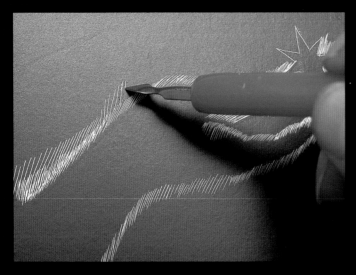

1 Three layers of parallel lines are used, one on top of the other, using different lengths, to create the impression of a graduated tone that becomes darker farther away from the arm. For larger areas a ruler can be used as a guide for straight lines.

2 To build up the impression of lighter tones, one set of parallel lines can then be crossed with another set. The tighter the mesh of lines, the lighter the apparent tone.

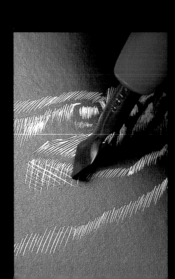

3 For the brightest areas, the surface can be completely removed to produce solid white. Do this gradually as the clay surface of the board is very thin, and you can go through to the backing board.

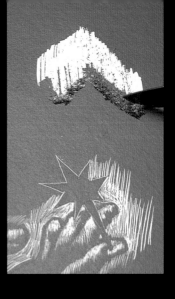

4 A whole variety of styles can be used with this medium, from tight technical drawings using fine ruled lines, to looser and bolder styles more reminiscent of woodcuts.

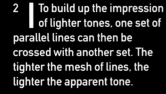

WHITE SCRAPERBOARD

White scraperboard is becoming increasingly popular with illustrators as it permits extensive areas of white in a design without the time-consuming task of removing them. However, it is advisable to work out your design beforehand, allowing you time to decide whether black or white scraperboard would be most appropriate.

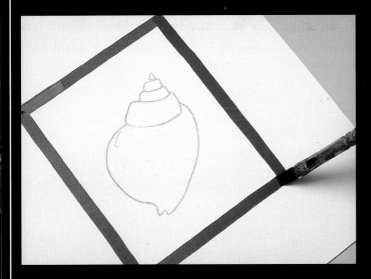

1 The design can either be applied freehand or using a tracing method. The areas of black are inked in using a brush and black India ink.

2 When applying the ink, you can leave small areas of white for highlights or, as in this case, lines used to accentuate the structure. Before working on the surface with any cutting tools, make sure the ink has dried thoroughly.

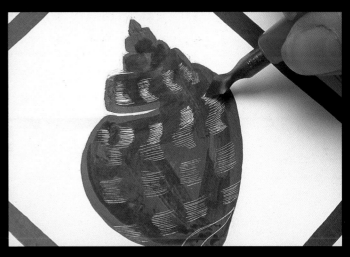

3 The same techniques used for black scraperboard can then be applied, with the same choice of tools creating different line effects.

4 A broad knife-blade cutter is used to create this geometric border pattern. As this is a very precise design, it is easy to make mistakes. Inevitably this happens to all of us, but it can be easily remedied by inking over the error and reworking it.

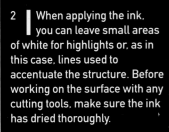

SPATTERING

Scraperboard lends itself effectively to fine detail. However, it can be extremely time-consuming to apply texture, particularly areas of random marks. Spattering will enable you to produce a fine random pattern very quickly.

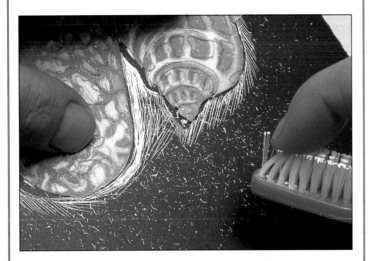

1 | After the image has been completed, a mask that accurately covers the area to be protected is cut from tracing paper. Using an old toothbrush dipped in white gouache or acrylic, the area is "spattered" by running a finger over the bristles.

2 | This process can be repeated until the intended coverage is achieved. This technique is extremely effective for producing interesting backgrounds and for mist, rain, and snow.

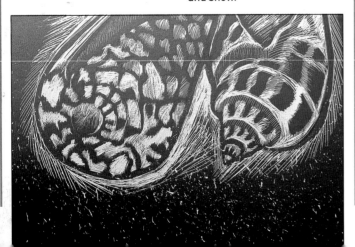

APPLYING COLOR

Color is perhaps a quality one does not always associate with scraperboard. However, it is extremely easy to apply, and it transforms this traditionally monochrome technique. In this case black scraperboard is used as a ground, but this technique works equally well on white scraperboard.

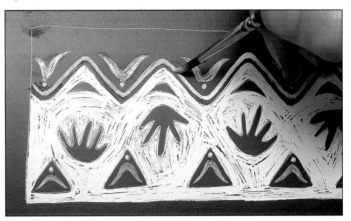

1 | The technique for the first part of the process is the same as for the traditional method. The paint is applied with a fine brush. Any water soluble medium is suitable, the most popular being watercolor and ink.

2 | The pigment sinks into the chalky surface and dries rapidly. Further colors are applied as desired to complete the illustration.

Tracing and transferring

TRACING IS AN EASILY LEARNED TECHNIQUE WHICH HAS AN EVERYDAY APPLICATION FOR THE ILLUSTRATOR. BECAUSE OF THE SHORT DEADLINES OF MOST COMMISSIONS, ILLUSTRATORS NEED TO FIND EVERY METHOD AVAILABLE TO HELP SPEED UP THE CREATIVE PROCESS.

By tracing around the outline of a design or image, it can be transferred quickly and easily to a new surface.

BASIC EQUIPMENT There are now a wide variety of different types of tracing and transfer paper. Tracing paper comes in different weights and degrees of transparency. Matt drafting film is preferable to tracing paper as it is dimensionally stable and not affected by moisture although more expensive. Transfer paper comes pre-coated on the reverse side, saving you from having to retrace your tracing to reverse the image.

Perhaps the most effective method of tracing involves the use of a light box. It cannot be stressed enough how useful this piece of equipment is for the working illustrator and, though expensive, it is a true investment. They can be bought in a variety of sizes, and a self-cooling mechanism is advised, or you roast and the paper curls up.

Masking tape for anchoring the tracing and a selection of graphite pencils are useful.

APPLICATIONS FOR THE ILLUSTRATOR Tracing is used by the illustrator in many ways. It is useful to the illustrator for copying the chosen image from a page of roughs to the paper of the finished work. Images can be traced from a sketchbook or magazine to be incorporated into illustrations, or part of a rejected image can be copied to a new surface.

GETTING STARTED When tracing, the image must not move under the paper, so it helps to hold the corners down with masking tape. Traditional tracing paper needs to be retraced with a pencil on the reverse, to transfer the image the correct way around. Transfer paper saves you from this arduous task and is used by placing it *under* your trace and drawing over the image. So a rough can be directly traced from the layout pad through the transfer paper onto the fresh surface.

The light box transmits an intense light, making it possible to trace through heavier papers such as watercolor paper. This works best when the original is on thin paper such as a layout pad and your finished artwork is destined for a less heavy paper such as NOT 90lb./190gsm. A clear, black reference image will help, too.

PAPERS
Tracing and transfer papers: traditional tracing paper ❶ 30 gsm ❷ 60 gsm ❸ 90 gsm. The higher the gsm the more opaque the paper. For fine detail work use fine paper; for bolder work or work where you are reusing the tracing paper use a heavier weight of paper. ❹ a detail showing white transfer paper.

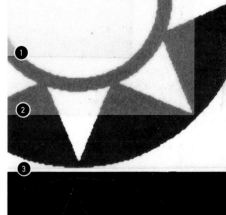
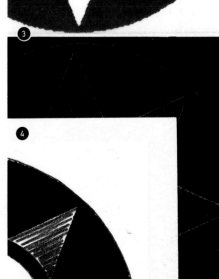

☞
Enlarging and Scaling up; Linework.

TRADITIONAL TRACING

We have all used this method of transferring an image from one source to another at one time or another, and it is still probably the simplest and cheapest. However, it can be a little time-consuming for the very busy illustrator.

1 ▌ If possible, anchor the original picture to a solid surface with masking tape. Now lay tracing paper on top and secure it with masking tape at three corners. This means you can peek underneath. Trace over the image in pencil.

2 ▌ Once the tracing is complete, remove the tracing paper. Now, on the reverse side, using a soft pencil, scribble roughly all over the image area.

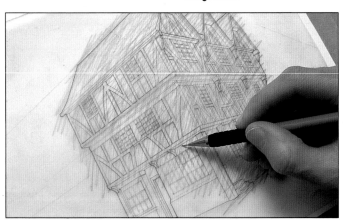

3 ▌ To make sure the whole area is covered with graphite, use a paper towel to smudge the pencil on the reverse side and fill any gaps.

4 ▌ Turning the tracing paper onto the right side, lay it on the new paper surface, anchoring it firmly again on three corners with masking tape. Retrace the image with a sharp pencil following your original. Use a ruler, if necessary, for any straight lines.

5 ▌ With the tracing attached only on three sides, you can look underneath to make sure that the lines are coming out dark enough and all the details have been traced through.

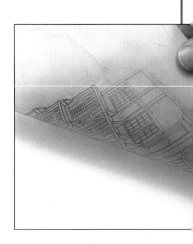

TRANSFER PAPER

Transfer paper is widely used by illustrators as it greatly speeds up the process of tracing. Most clients wish to see a pencil sketch, or rough, before giving the go-ahead for finished artwork, so that they can make changes if they wish. The new layout will then need to be transferred onto the paper being used for finished artwork.

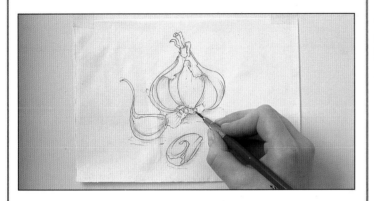

1 | The design is first sketched out on layout paper, following the client's brief. If it is to be faxed to the client, make sure it is dark enough to be picked up by the machine.

2 | Once the client has agreed the design, place the layout over the artwork paper with the transfer paper sandwiched in between, graphite surface down. Make sure your design and the artwork paper are both firmly held down with masking tape, before retracing the design.

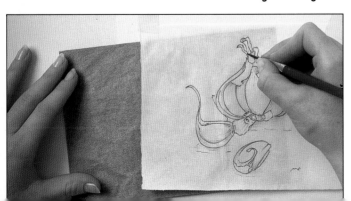

LIGHT BOX

This is probably the simplest method for tracing, and for the busy illustrator the expense can be justified by increased speed and quality. The two previous methods are very effective, but the line produced on the artwork paper is not as fine as an original line made by a pencil. It is also difficult to show variations in line, which is easy using the light box.

1 | The original design is sketched out onto layout paper. This must be done using a dark line, or rendered with a marker. The rough is then placed on the light box and held with masking tape.

2 | The artwork paper is then placed over the top. The heavier the paper, the more difficult it is to see through. When the light is switched on, your design will be visible for you to trace through, direct onto the artwork paper.

Watercolor

WATERCOLOR IS ONE OF THE MOST BEAUTIFUL AND EXPRESSIVE PAINTING MEDIA. AS THERE ARE SO MANY VARIED TECHNIQUES TO USE, IT IS EASY TO DEVELOP A DISTINCTIVE STYLE.

The main characteristic of watercolor is that it is transparent and can be used very wet. The pigment is used in various stages of dilution, known as washes, and the brilliance of the white paper is allowed to shine through the palest washes and for highlights.

BASIC EQUIPMENT Watercolors can be bought dried, in pans, or wet, in tubes, in a wide range of colors. Buy a few to start with and add more as you need them.

When using watercolor, it is very important to choose the paper which best suits your style. The wetter and looser your style, the rougher the paper texture needs to be and the heavier the weight. It is best to start with an average weight, such as NOT 140lb./300gsm, then try out rougher and smoother papers until you find one that suits your style. Paper can be bought in loose sheets or pads, ready to stretch or pre-stretched.

Sable brushes are the best, though a little expensive, but only a few sizes are really needed. The higher the number, the larger the brush. Recommended sizes are a No. 3 for more detailed work and No. 8 for larger washes. Other useful items are: a small sponge, masking fluid, white gouache, and paper towels.

APPLICATIONS FOR THE ILLUSTRATOR Because of its flexibility, watercolor can be used for all subjects, from highly expressive abstract work to very detailed technical subjects. It gives a brilliant but slightly fragile look, and is therefore not suitable for modeling form opaquely and solidly, where gouache and acrylic are more suitable media. As watercolor is a subtle medium, the color can be difficult to reproduce faithfully in the printing process. Natural pigments can be difficult to pick up accurately using the cheaper methods of reproduction. This can be overcome by using the new breed of watercolors which use manufactured pigments that can be picked up more accurately by the modern laser reproduction processes.

GETTING STARTED Watercolor is a friendly medium for beginners, but it is a difficult one to master. The most important thing to remember with watercolor is that you work from light to dark, using the white of the paper for the highlights. The amount of paint in relation to the amount of water determines the lightness or darkness of the color. Dilute layers can be applied one over the other to build up the dark areas. As the rendering needs to be done quickly and precisely, it is important to work out your composition accurately before applying the pigment. Start with subjects that rely on looseness of detail and texture, such as skies, simple landscapes, and objects such as fruit, where you can have fun experimenting.

Stephanie Hawken
The artist has made combined wet-in-wet washes with crisp definition worked wet-on-dry. Small highlights are reserved as pale washes.

☞
Corrections; Enlarging and Scaling up.

PAPER TEXTURES

Watercolor paper is made in different weights and textures. Because watercolor techniques rely so much on the texture of paper, it is important to choose the best one for your own style.

❶ As its name suggests, watercolor board is watercolor paper attached to board. It is very useful when you have no time to stretch paper.

❷ Not. This term is short for "not hot pressed." The paper has a gently textured surface.
❸ Rough paper is suitable for broad, expressive work and wet washes.
❹ Hot-pressed paper has a smooth surface, making it ideal for highly detailed work.
❺ & ❻ Handmade papers are produced in all kinds of textures, making them great fun to experiment with.

STRETCHING PAPER

Paper has a truly infuriating tendency to buckle when water is applied to the surface, particularly on lighter-weight papers. When you are trying to produce an illustration, this does not enhance its professional appearance. By stretching your paper, you will remove any possibility of producing a wrinkled piece of work.

1 Watercolor paper is one-sided, and it is very important that you remember which is the top side—initially the watermark will show you. Using clean cold water, immerse the paper completely for a few minutes.

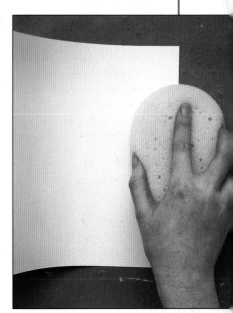

2 The paper is then laid good side up onto a clean wooden drawing board. Lay the paper down, starting at one edge and pressing it across. Using a clean sponge, stroke the paper in one direction to remove any air bubbles between the paper and the board.

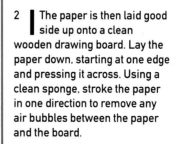

3 Remove any excess water with a squeezed-out dry sponge and then seal the edges of the paper with gummed tape. Tear a length a little longer than one side of the paper and, to activate the glue, stroke it with the wet sponge. Do not under- or oversoak it.

4 Lay the strip so that it covers the edge of the paper. Repeat for all four sides. Small corner pieces can be added at the end to prevent the strip from lifting at the corners once it is dry.

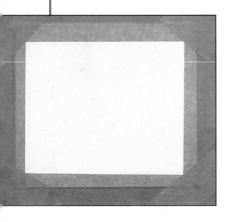

5 Leave the paper to dry in a warm place. The paper must be totally dry before it is used. This is a lengthy process and, for the busy illustrator, blocks of prestretched paper are a much quicker, though more expensive, option.

MIXING COLORS

When you use watercolors, the most important consideration is how much pigment to mix with how much water. Beginners often use too much paint, which causes their work to look heavy and dull.

1 There are two main techniques for mixing watercolor. Paint can be put in a mixing palette and water can be added, which means you can fine-tune the colors.

2 In the more traditional method, layers of transparent color are applied directly on the paper, one over the other. Thus the colors are optically mixed.

WET-IN-WET

As you will be working with lots of water, there is a risk of the paper buckling. To prevent this, either use a heavy paper—at least 160lbs./340gsm—or stretch the paper. Rough textures give the best results. Use large brushes to deliver the maximum amount of pigment and water.

1 Draw your image faintly with a pencil, then fill the brush and wet the whole area inside the outline. You need to be accurate to achieve a clean edge.

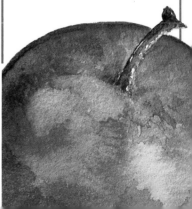

DRY BRUSHING

Dry brushing can be used either on its own or over the top of flat washes. Here, the technique is used on its own to render exquisitely fine detail. Although a slow process, it is a style often used by scientific illustrators. When applied over washes, it is ideal for producing textures such as grass and fur. Dry brush is not restricted to watercolor and can be used with gouache and acrylic.

This technique is particularly well suited to rendering fine detail.

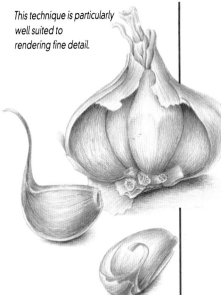

2 ▌ The color is added in layers, starting with the palest washes and allowing the pigment to mix on the paper. Keep in mind where you wish the highlights to be, and work the dark areas around them.

4 ▌ Try to keep the whole area as wet as possible by using very watery washes. This helps the layers to mix softly without leaving hard edges.

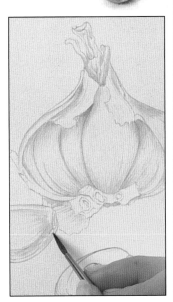

3 ▌ If you add too much pigment, it can be removed by lightly dabbing with a small piece of dry paper towel.

5 ▌ The shadow is added at the end. If the image is still wet, the colors will bleed into the shadow; but if it is allowed to dry first, they will remain separate.

1 ▌ The outline is made lightly in pencil onto a very smooth paper or board. Then the pencil lines are painted over using a fine brush.

2 ▌ The most important aspect of this style is that the brush is used very dry. Each layer of color is built up with interlocking lines, starting with the palest colors.

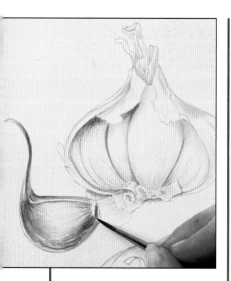

3 Once one layer is completed and dry, the next darker layer can be added. The danger lies in adding too many layers, thus ending up with a muddied, overworked illustration.

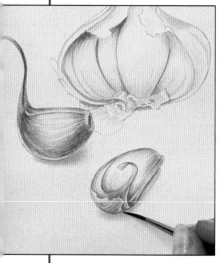

4 The best results can be achieved by simplifying the tonal areas – highlight, mid-tone and shadow – only applying new colors to certain areas.

MIXED WATERCOLOR TECHNIQUE

There are probably as many ways of using watercolor as there are illustrators. The following sequence shows what is probably the most traditional method, that of building up the image with a mixture of dry brush and washes, or glazes.

1 The paper here is 140lb./ 300gsm NOT surface, and the brush is a No. 3 sable. The image is first drawn in lightly with a medium-soft pencil such as an HB.

The pigment can also be bought in porcelain pans.

2 To build up the form of the onion, pale washes are used, with the color applied to the outside edge first, and then tempted into the middle with water only on the brush. This achieves a graduated tone.

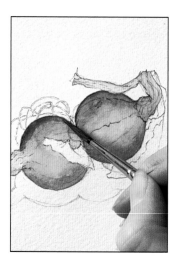

3 While the wash is still wet, more pigment added to the edges will naturally bleed into the middle. You can also mix different colors.

4 When the wash is dry, detail can be added using a drier brush and more concentrated paint, which is the method used for the lines on the onion. A smaller brush may be useful at this point.

5 Shadows and highlights are added last. Payne's gray, a useful color for shadows, was applied as a very wet wash all at once, to avoid unevenness. For the gentle highlight, white gouache is used, and the edges are softened with a wet brush.

6 This step may be seen as minor cheating, but drawing over watercolor with pencil is very effective for rendering tiny detail and crisping up the edges of a wash. Make sure that the pencil is sharp and only use it sparingly.

7 The key to making objects appear realistically solid is to use strong tonal differences, that is, make the dark areas very dark and the light ones very light. To help you identify the tones, look at the subject through half-closed eyes.

SCRATCHING OUT

Illustrators have to work to tight deadlines, so techniques that can speed up your work can be very handy. Keeping small areas for white highlights can be difficult when you are working at speed. Scratching out with a blade after the paint has dried is a quick and effective method of reclaiming highlights. Alternative methods are the use of opaque white paint such as gouache, or masking fluid applied before the color is laid on.

1 This technique is particularly suitable for fine-line highlights. It should only be used on heavier papers, 140lbs. /300gsm or over, as it is possible to make holes in thin ones.

2 For straight lines, a little metal ruler is useful to guide your hand. Drag the scalpel lightly at first, repeating the process until you achieve the amount of highlight required.

3 The point of the scalpel has given a fine white line. For larger areas and diffused highlights, you can use a round-ended knife, or drag a razor blade over the surface.

SPONGING

Sponging is a very expressive method that is quick to master. It is ideal for experimentation. It can be used as a method on its own, to build a complete image, or combined with other watercolor techniques.

1 A small natural sponge is the ideal tool for this technique. It is used quite dry on a rough-surfaced paper to produce a highly textured effect.

A marvelous tool for applying very wet washes.

2 | Each color is applied separately, with each application allowed to dry, and the sponge well washed between stages. The pressure can be varied to squeeze more or less pigment onto the paper.

3 | Once each wash has dried, more colors or tones can be overlaid, as with the tree here. This helps to create a more three-dimensional form.

4 | The great value of this technique is that it creates a complete image that is both evocative and decorative in a very short time, always a bonus for the busy illustrator.

If tape is too tacky, it may tear your paper. To avoid this, stick the strip to the inside of your arm before applying it.

MASKING

Masking tape can be used for crisp edges around your illustration. When using fine hot-pressed papers, take care when removing the tape or you may damage the paper.

1 | Before the masking tape is applied, measure the dimensions of your illustration using a set square, and pencil in lightly. Now carefully lay down the masking tape only pressing down the inside edge, taking particular care at the corners. Next add the wash as usual.

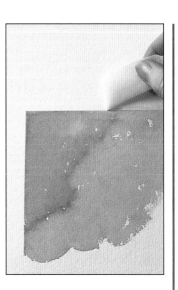

2 | Make sure that the wash is completely dry before removing the tape. Each strip is lifted off separately and slowly, taking care not to tear the paper.

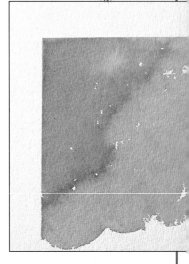

3 | The result is clean and crisp. If the paint does seep under the tape, scratch it out with a scalpel.

Wood engraving

THIS IS A RELIEF PRINTING TECHNIQUE SIMILAR TO WOODCUT, BUT BECAUSE THE BLOCK IS CUT FROM THE END GRAIN, IT IS POSSIBLE TO PRODUCE MUCH FINER DETAIL. A GRAVER IS THE TOOL USED TO INCISE THE IMAGE INTO THE WOOD.

BASIC EQUIPMENT The blocks are usually bought ready-prepared and can be expensive. Boxwood is most commonly used, but cherry and pear are also suitable. These woods have extremely hard surfaces, allowing the artist to create detailed images using very fine lines.

The tools used for wood engraving are made from fine-quality tempered steel with a wooden handle. They are sharpened into different shapes to provide a variety of cutting tips. These tools must be kept sharp and should not leave a burl (burr) on the surface.

To make the block easier to control when producing curved lines, it is placed on an engraver's sandbag. Having the block raised off the work bench also helps you to maintain a firmer grip. The ink can be applied with a small rubber roller. As the detail produced is so fine, the printing ink should be quite dry to prevent flooding the delicate marks. The prints can be hand-burnished with the bowl of a spoon rubbed on the reverse of the paper. As with other relief printing methods, the paper should be slightly absorbent.

APPLICATIONS FOR THE ILLUSTRATOR This is a specialized technique for the advanced print-maker. A small number of contemporary artists use this method for book illustration, but more often they appear as limited-edition prints.

GETTING STARTED Wood engraving is a most demanding technique, but the final results can be like little jewels.

The image is drawn directly onto the wood with a soft graphite pencil and is then fixed. It can be helpful to ink the surface of the block, before engraving as it helps you to visualize the finished effect. It is important to find your own method of holding the block, which varies for each individual. The graver is held with the handle in the palm of your hand, your thumb resting on the block to steady the blade and keep it at the correct angle. Practice on a resin block, which is much cheaper than boxwood, so mistakes don't matter so much. Make parallel lines and hatching first, before moving on to curved lines.

When inking the block, roll it only once in each direction to prevent over-inking. The impression is then made, burnishing the image onto the paper from the back with the spoon. Having taken the impression, you can clean the ink off the block and add more detail until you are satisfied with the image.

Roland Stringer
This dramatic image was created by first using large areas of solid black to create a silhouette, onto which detail was added.

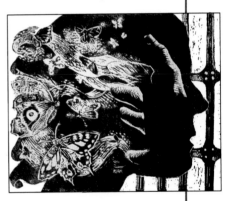

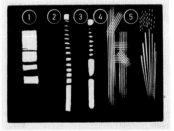

Etching; Linoleumcut and Woodcut; Scraperboard.

MARK MAKING
Each wood-engraving tool creates a very different mark.
❶ chisel, ❷ square scorper,
❸ round scorper, ❹ multiple,
❺ tint tool, ❻ bullsticker,
❼ spitsticker, ❽ graver.

The engraving tools are fine shafts of metal faceted and sharpened to form various shapes of cutting tip. The main types are the lozenge-shaped graver for general line work; the elliptical spitsticker, designed for cutting curves; the squared or rounded scorper, used for broad marks and clearing areas of the block; and the fine tint tool, which maintains a line of uniform width.

TRACING THE IMAGE

You can draw an image directly onto the block with a soft pencil. If, however, you are a little uncertain of your design, it is possible to trace it. Darkening the block all over with black ink will help you appreciate how your design will look when printed. Remember that your illustration will eventually print in reverse, so be careful if you are using lettering.

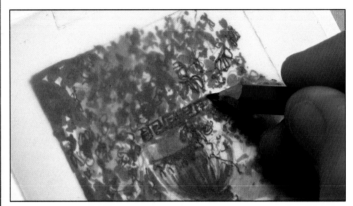

1 | In this example the illustrator has used traditional tracing paper. However, a successful alternative is white carbon paper. Using a sketch or a more finished pen and ink drawing, the image is traced on to the tracing paper.

2 | Place the tracing face down on the block and secure it with tape. If you are using lettering in your design, this method allows you to make sure the lettering is reversed so it prints correctly.

3 | Using an HB pencil, firmly rub over the whole design. The pressure should transfer the graphite onto the block. Regularly lift the tracing from time to time to check that you are using enough pressure.

Transferring an existing image onto the block can be done quickly and simply using tracing and transfer papers.

INKING IN

As pencil marks can smudge easily, it is important to fix your image with spray fixative as soon as possible. Alternatively, as in this example, the design can be inked in.

| To ink in a design, use a dip pen with a fine drawing nib and black India ink. Carefully follow the outlines of your original design.

SHARPENING TOOLS

It is extremely important to keep your tools as sharp as possible, if you are to retain the fine quality of line traditionally associated with wood engraving. Sharpening is done on an oilstone, which comes in three grades: course, medium, and fine. If you make sure your tools never become blunt, the fine grade is all you will need.

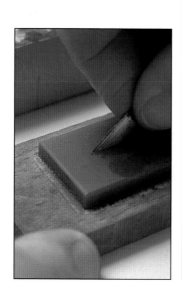

| Use a little oil for lubrication, then turn the tool from side to side, pushing the tool up and down with a gentle rolling action. This method is suitable for all gouges, except those that are V-shaped, where each cutting edge is sharpened separately, making sure that the V stays symmetrical.

ENGRAVING THE IMAGE

Every engraver will devise his or her own method of holding tools. The important thing to remember is that the graver and wood must be held firmly. The angle of the cut should be shallow, so the graver is held at an obtuse angle to the block, using the thumb resting on the wood to maintain the blade at the correct angle.

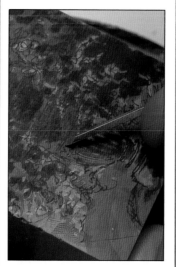

| Traditionally an engraver's sandbag is used to rest the wood on. This allows the block to be turned easily with the free hand rather than by moving your hand. This allows you to produce gentler curved lines.

Wood-engraving techniques enable the artist to create fine line detail and intricate textures.

PRINTING

As the lines produced with the graving tools are very fine, it is vital to use the correct consistency of ink. If it is too runny, it will fill the fine lines, resulting in a bad print.

1 | A glass mixing slab is used to roll out the ink. Make sure that it is clean and free of dust. This example clearly demonstrates the correct consistency of ink.

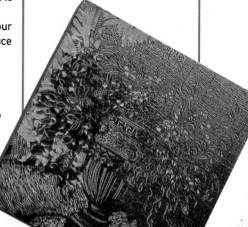

2 A small hard rubber or plastic roller is best. If the roller is too soft, it will tend to fill in the lines. Roll out the ink until it forms a thin consistent layer.

3 The roller needs only to be applied once in each direction as over-inking will also fill in the delicate lines, resulting in a bad print. Alternatively, the ink can be applied with a brush or leather dabber.

MAKING A REGISTRATION FRAME

This is a useful aid for all forms of printing as it allows you to produce multicolored prints by overlaying impressions from separate blocks accurately. For engraving techniques, it makes it possible to align the image on the paper in exactly the same place for each print. In this example the frame is quite a complicated structure, but as long as your block remains the same thickness, it can be reused.

1 Three cardboard frames are made, at different heights, for the top left-hand corner. The outer one slightly higher than the middle, which is at the same height as the block. Thin slivers of cardboard are then placed at the bottom of the outer frame.

2 The block is placed inside the inner frame, making sure it rests hard against the edge. This inner frame controls the distance of the image from the edge of the paper, therefore the wider this frame, the farther the image is from the edge.

3 The printing paper is then placed inside the outer frame. This process means that on each occasion the image remains at exactly the same distance from the edge of the paper, essential if you are producing a series of prints.

This little gadget will help you to produce identical prints. Creating a guide for placing the paper over the block ensures that all the imprints will appear in the same position on the paper.

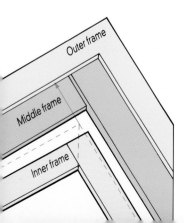

BURNISHING

Pressure is needed to transfer the image from the block onto the paper. Professionally this is done on a flat-bed press, but it is possible to produce prints by hand-printing techniques, such as burnishing. Printing paper needs to be thin and absorbent, but to achieve a black velvety print, dampen the paper between two layers of wet newspaper.

1 Burnishing can be done with the back of a spoon, or in this case a round-ended wooden spatula. The printing paper is covered with a thicker piece of paper, and the burnishing tool is rubbed over the surface in a circular motion from the center outward.

2 The print is then carefully peeled off the block from one corner. If at this stage before it is removed totally, the print is not distinct enough, it can be carefully replaced on the block for further burnishing.

3 Another method possible at home is to use a small hand press. Alternatively, when you have prepared your block and taken hand-printed proofs, time can be booked at a print studio, where you can make professional-quality prints.

GOING PROFESSIONAL

Whether you are leaving college or have decided to give up a staff job to go freelance, there comes a point when you have to take a fresh look at your portfolio and your attitude toward your work.

The right attitude is critical. As a professional you have to view your work as a product. For most illustrators this can be very tough, as it is difficult to become detached from something that demands blood, sweat, and tears. However it is vital for the professional illustrator not to be precious about his or her work, as this can cause major problems with clients. The maxim, "The client is always right," applies to our profession as to many others, and difficult illustrators will find that they have very few regular clients.

If you are to be a successful illustrator it is essential that you consider yourself as a business person first and an artist second. This means that you are always punctual for interviews, are well organized, always meet deadlines, and, most important, send out your invoices as quickly as possible. Gaining the respect of your clients is essential and can be easily achieved if you stick to these few simple rules.

Hudson

Hudson, Strumpfmode für Damen, Herren und

Sie haben die *Beine.*
Wir die *Mode.*

PORTFOLIOS
When putting together a portfolio, you need to show clients the very best of your work. For tips on presenting a portfolio, turn to page 132.

BRIEFS

Some designers give very loose briefs, leaving all the creative input up to the illustrator; others like to specify exactly what they want. Either way, you need to learn how to interpret a brief correctly. Work produced to the standard shown on this page is only good if it pleases the client.

Briefs and contract terms

GOOD COMMUNICATION BETWEEN CLIENT AND ILLUSTRATOR WILL RESULT IN A SUCCESSFUL JOB. TO AVOID ANY MISUNDERSTANDINGS, IT IS VITAL THAT BOTH PARTIES KNOW WHAT IS DEMANDED OF EACH.

Once the illustrator has been commissioned for a job, certain details must be negotiated, the most important being the fee. Some companies will have a set fee that will be included in their overall budget, or they may ask for a quote.

When working out the fee for a job the main points to consider are:

● How long will it take to do? Roughly work out the number of hours and decide on a per hourly rate. This will then be the minimum charge.

● Who is the client? The bigger the client the larger the budget; take this into consideration when deciding on your hourly rate.

● What are they buying? You will need to ask them this. The variations are: One-use copyright; extra usage on other products; complete ownership of copyright; ownership of artwork.

Unless otherwise agreed, the ownership of both the artwork and copyright resides with the artist, if the client wishes to buy more than limited rights, they have to pay for it. No one may reuse your work without your permission.

● What will your costs be? You will need to include all your general studio costs as well as any special costs the job may incur: Rent; telephone; materials; postage.

This amount can then be added to each job, making sure to amend it if the situation demands.

Try not to be pressed into giving a quote immediately; explain that you need time to work it out. However, you must do this promptly, as you may lose the client if you delay. Once the amount has been agreed it can be put in writing and included with your terms and conditions.

Most large companies will have a contract which they will ask you to sign before starting a job. Read it carefully and only sign it if you are completely happy. It can be the smaller companies, however, that are more difficult to deal with, especially if they have had little experience with design projects. In these situations it is advisable to have a contract containing all your terms and conditions. Ask them to sign a copy and return it before you start the job, as this can save a lot of heartache.

BRIEFS There are as many ways of briefing an illustrator as there are clients. Some clients may depend on your artistic ability to develop the artwork and therefore only supply the basic concept, whereas others hold your hand, thus enabling them to obtain their desired final image. The illustrator has to be flexible to each individual client's way of working, but most important, making sure that you both have the same ideas at the end of the day.

BRIEFING CHECKLIST

● **When is the deadline and can I realistically meet it?**
● **What is the budget for the job?**
● **Am I sure what the client wants?**
● **Have I got all the reference material needed for the job?**
● **Has the client approved my rough?**
● **Have I got all the necessary materials?**
● **How much time have I got to finish?**
● **How will I deliver it to make sure it is insured?**
● **Have I enclosed the invoice?**
● **Have they paid me?**

GOOD BRIEF

A good brief is one that includes all the information needed to complete the job without the need to contact the designer with numerous queries. An excellent brief will also include relevant reference material.

1 A commissioning letter that clearly explains the number of illustrations required.

2 A list of commissioned illustrations and titles.

3 A sheet of rough but accurate thumbnails for the designs, numbered and titled, and giving size and bleed.

4 Designer's layout showing how the artwork will look in context.

5 A design sheet showing layout possibilities for creating bleed needed on each illustration.

BAD BRIEF

Perhaps this phrase is a little too damning, as a sketchy brief does have the advantage of allowing you more scope for creativity. The only really "bad" brief is one that is misleading.

1 A rather vague commissioning letter that gives very little detail of what the designer really needs, and mentions no deadline.

2 A poor-quality, virtually unreadable black-and-white photocopy—no help to the illustrator.

3 A very sketchy drawing that gives very little idea of correct position or design.

1

10th Aug '96
Ref: AOI/ARI

...es,

...d enclosed a purchase order and a brief for "Reptile ...strations.

...al I need 19 symbols, render these in black only. The ease of ...mbol requires 10 variants, which accommodate a scale of ...the palm of the hand, 1 for simple, 10 for difficult (see ... Please note that as the symbols appear on both the left, ...ht sides of the page you will have to do two versions, one ...e bleed on the left, the other, with it on the right. Sheet B ...two possible ways of approaching this, either put the bleed ...overlay, or if doing the job electronically save the symbol ...fferent version and make any necessary alterations to the ...file.

...Whichever, make sure that the image in the square is flipped ...zontally, where it needs to be. If doing the job electronically ... each symbol as a separate document that is Quark compatible. ...On the following pages is a list of symbols required. I would ... to see roughs by the 18th, please call if you have any queries.

...gards

...lizabeth

Enc.

2

1. Globe/world map, to suggest location.
2. Length: metric (imperial) units
3. Environment: woodland temperate, woodland tropical, savannah, desert, aquatic and semi aquatic
4. Tank design
5. Sociability: agree in groups/ may eat smaller companions/ aggressive
6. Feeding: insectivorous/carnivorous/ vegetarian/omnivorous
7. Reproduction:...

3

4

5

BAD BRIEF side

1

Dear Joanna,

10th Aug '96
Ref: AOI/ARI

Please find enclosed a purchase order and a brief for the "Clove of Garlic" illustration.

I've sketched at the bottom of the page the sort of thing I'd like. However if you have any better ideas about the composition, then I'm open to suggestions. I thought maybe a watercolour would be nice, but then again you might have alternative suggestions for that too.

Perhaps you could show me some roughs over the next couple of weeks or so?

Regards

Elizabeth

Enc.

2

STARTERS AND SNACKS

BRUSCHETTA *with* ROASTED VEGETABLES

3

STARTERS AND SNACKS

TAGLIATELLE *with* GARLIC, OLIVE OIL, BASIL *and* PINE NUTS

Preparation, research, sources

"BE PREPARED!" AS MOST ILLUSTRATORS HAVE TO WORK TO EXTREMELY TIGHT DEADLINES, THERE IS OFTEN VERY LITTLE TIME TO RESEARCH REFERENCE MATERIAL.

To have an extensive library of books and other reference material is essential. You will find that this may build up naturally over the years, but if you are just starting out you may have to invest in a small resource library, particularly if you are a technical illustrator, i.e. medical, botanical, or mechanical.

Illustrators find that they become magpies, collecting old birthday and Christmas cards, bits of miscellaneous packaging, fallen leaves, teddy bears, blue-and-white china, buttons, bird nests, and any other interesting items, as you never know just what might come in useful for the next job.

When a commission arrives it is often difficult to come up with a new creative idea; this is where an inspirational source book can come in extremely handy. All of us find that there are certain images and materials that help stimulate our creative juices. These can be collected together into a sketch book or file, and this can then act as a starting-off point for when you are feeling particularly divest of creative ideas. You will know for yourself what these are, but for instance, a beautifully designed wine label, a small snip of fabric, an old faded piece of wall paper, or a holiday photograph of the colors and textures of a crumbling wall in Tuscany.

WORKING METHODS
While most artists prefer to work from life, illustrators rely on reference – and lots of it.

Working from reference: Build up a library of good reference books, magazine features, models, pinned insects, anything that you can use as reference in your illustration.

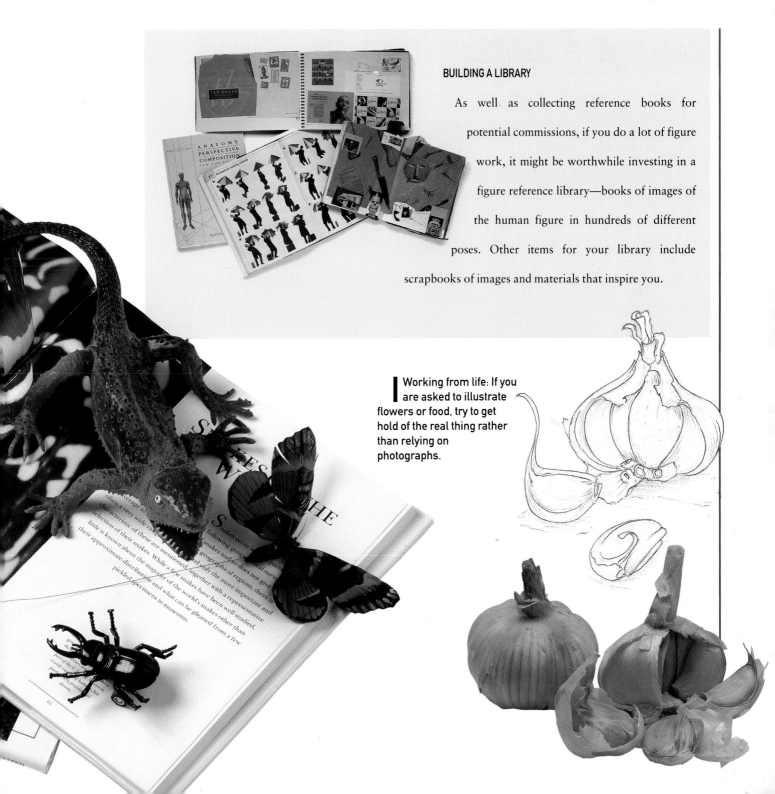

BUILDING A LIBRARY

As well as collecting reference books for potential commissions, if you do a lot of figure work, it might be worthwhile investing in a figure reference library—books of images of the human figure in hundreds of different poses. Other items for your library include scrapbooks of images and materials that inspire you.

Working from life: If you are asked to illustrate flowers or food, try to get hold of the real thing rather than relying on photographs.

Roughs and visuals

IT IS OFTEN VERY DIFFICULT FOR THE CLIENT AND THE ILLUSTRATOR TO VISUALIZE THE COMPLETED ILLUSTRATION, BUT THIS IS WHERE A CLEAR ROUGH OR VISUAL WILL HELP BOTH.

Once you have collected all the relevant reference material together, do some rough sketches on a layout pad, to work out the general composition of your illustration. Try to keep the drawing as rough and lively as possible; any fine-tuning can then be done by tracing the design through onto further sheets of layout paper. This is an extremely successful method, enabling you to produce the finished design without losing the energy of the first sketch.

Most clients will automatically ask to see a rough or visual of the illustration and possibly give you a deadline for this section of the job. If they don't ask, for your own sake it is advisable to supply one, as this will prevent any misunderstandings occurring which could lead to their rejecting your finished work. Normally, all they will wish to see is a black-and-white outline, although for particular jobs they may ask for a color one. If so remember to take this into account in your pricing of the job.

If the deadline is very tight it is advisable to fax your roughs as mailing them might take a few days. But remember, if your pencil rough is a little pale it will not fax properly; either use a very soft pencil to make your roughs darker, or take a photocopy first to produce a darker image. Photocopying can also be a useful process when having to reduce large work to fax, but make sure you include the original dimensions on your work, so it can be scaled up later.

You may find calling the client soon after sending the fax will help you get a quick response to your work. It is vital that you get their go-ahead before you progress to the final artwork.

The client may ask you to make some changes to your original design. This can often be a little upsetting to the new illustrator, but don't feel that it is a rejection of your work, try to see that you and the designer are working as a team to produce the best illustration for the job.

FROM ROUGH TO FINISHED ARTWORK

The job of a rough, or visual, is to provide your client with a key outline of your design.

1 The illustrator has used a lively sketch that shows the client she has understood their brief. Extra detail takes time and can be wasted effort if the client makes changes.

2 In this case the client was happy with the sketch and the illustrator was able to complete the job from her original design. Note that in the rough she indicated the position of the type, and in the finished illustration has reduced the intensity of color in this area.

PANTONE®
2706 C

PANTONE®
2736 C

PANTONE®
141 C

© PANTONE, Inc

You may be asked to make the artwork suitable for reproduction at several different sizes (below). This is done at the reproduction stage, so you don't have to produce any extra artwork. If you find that an illustration is reused and applied to other printed matter, make sure that this was budgeted for in the original quote.

APPLICATIONS

It is important to understand how your work changes when it is reproduced, as this will help you develop your style and technique for printing. There are many techniques used in the industry for reproduction and printing, some better than others, so always look closely at the finished results of your work.

❶ Create a wide variation of tone in the original, as subtle gradations can be lost in reproduction

❷ Consider where type will be dropped into the illustration and design your work accordingly

❸ Reduction gives a stronger appearance to the work, so work larger than the finished printed piece

❹ Some colors can change quite drastically when printed, particularly yellows, so try to keep them bright. Some illustrators send Pantone colors along with their artwork when dealing direct with the printer

Delivery

ENSURING THAT YOUR WORK ARRIVES WITH
YOUR CLIENT SAFELY AND ON TIME, IS
ONE OF THE ILLUSTRATOR'S GREATEST
NIGHTMARES.

When preparing your work for delivery, there are two main considerations—good presentation and good protection. The standard way of presenting artwork is on a sheet of black mounting card that is slightly larger than your illustration. Always leave a wide margin of surplus paper around your composition (never name or date your work near the illustration), and tack it by the two top corners to the board with low tack or magic tape. A cover sheet of either tracing or layout paper is then laid over the top and secured at the back with masking tape. Finally, a protective layer of black sugar paper is applied in the same way. It may seem an elaborate procedure, but it will protect your artwork. The transparent sheet is provided for the designer to add instructions to the printer.

On the front cover it is advisable to display your name, address, and telephone number. This can be done quickly by attaching a pre-printed business card. This serves a number of purposes: it will give the correct spelling of your name for your illustration credit and make sure that your artwork returns to the correct address.

Before you put the presentation board into an envelope it is advisable, particularly in winter, to wrap it in plastic, as this will prevent it from getting wet in transit. The best envelopes to use are the ones with a cardboard backing. To make the illustration extra safe, turn the presentation board so the image faces this hard surface, or alternatively add an extra sheet, sandwiching it in between the two. Enclose with your illustration a compliment slip attached to your invoice and any other paperwork such as purchase orders and covering letters. Seal the envelope with parcel tape; this can also be applied to the corners to give them extra protection. It is also a good idea to write your name and address on the reverse of the envelope and in large red letters on the front, "Art Work Do Not Bend."

Don't forget that it will take time to send your package, so build this element into your time schedule for the whole job. If it is a particularly tight deadline you may find that your client will be prepared to pay for a courier. This can be arranged either by them or by you if you already know of a good one, but don't forget to put this extra expense onto the invoice.

If you are to send your work by ordinary mail, find out how much it will be insured for. You will find that there are a variety of ways to register and insure your package, so make sure that you choose the most suitable.

TAPES AND WRAPPING

There is nothing more frustrating than completing a job that has to be delivered promptly and finding you have no brown paper or parcel tape. Make sure you always have the right packaging materials for any job.

1. Parcel tape, strong, waterproof, and highly adhesive
2. Masking tape is multi-purposed, useful for attaching cover papers.
3. Low-tack tape is essential for attaching artwork.
4. Cardboard roll, useful for artwork rendered on flimsy paper.
5. Brown paper for wrapping.
6. Protective bubble wrap.

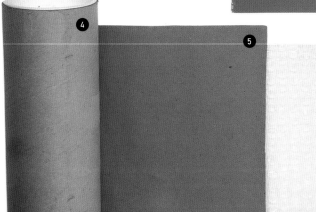

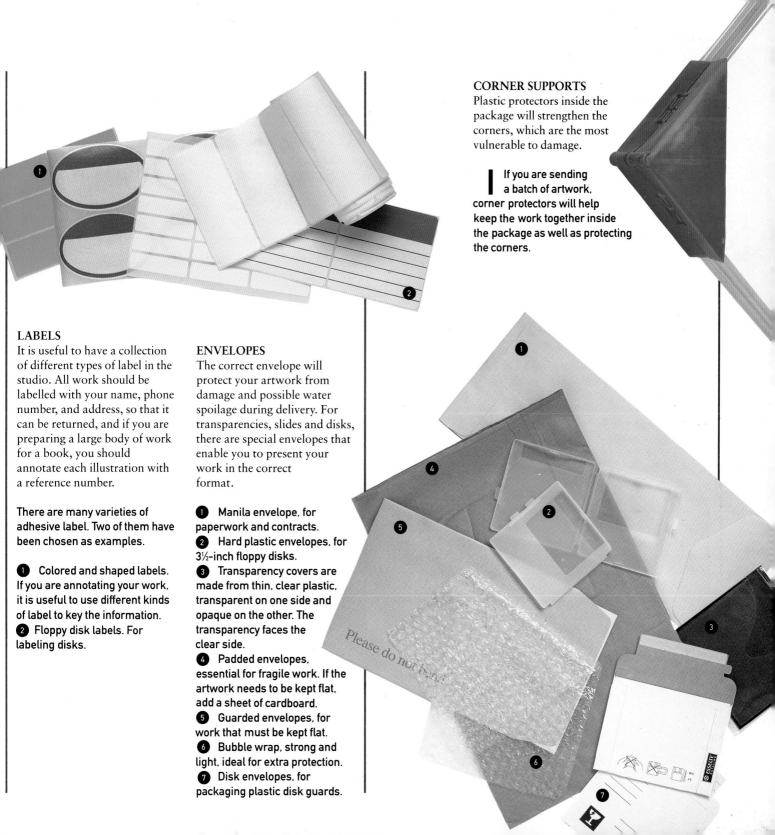

CORNER SUPPORTS

Plastic protectors inside the package will strengthen the corners, which are the most vulnerable to damage.

If you are sending a batch of artwork, corner protectors will help keep the work together inside the package as well as protecting the corners.

LABELS

It is useful to have a collection of different types of label in the studio. All work should be labelled with your name, phone number, and address, so that it can be returned, and if you are preparing a large body of work for a book, you should annotate each illustration with a reference number.

There are many varieties of adhesive label. Two of them have been chosen as examples.

1 Colored and shaped labels. If you are annotating your work, it is useful to use different kinds of label to key the information.
2 Floppy disk labels. For labeling disks.

ENVELOPES

The correct envelope will protect your artwork from damage and possible water spoilage during delivery. For transparencies, slides and disks, there are special envelopes that enable you to present your work in the correct format.

1 Manila envelope, for paperwork and contracts.
2 Hard plastic envelopes, for 3½-inch floppy disks.
3 Transparency covers are made from thin, clear plastic, transparent on one side and opaque on the other. The transparency faces the clear side.
4 Padded envelopes, essential for fragile work. If the artwork needs to be kept flat, add a sheet of cardboard.
5 Guarded envelopes, for work that must be kept flat.
6 Bubble wrap, strong and light, ideal for extra protection.
7 Disk envelopes, for packaging plastic disk guards.

Choosing your market

BEFORE MAKING YOUR CHOICE, STUDY THE MARKET TO ESTABLISH WHAT YOUR WORK IS MOST SUITED FOR.

Knowing the markets that regularly commission illustration will help you to judge which areas to target with your own work, so it is worth spending time researching, which involves keeping your eyes open at all times. When you are shopping in the supermarket, you will see different examples of food packaging, always a strong market. When you open a book or magazine, you will notice that each publisher has subjects or styles that they favor. Even when you play a CD or tape, you may see illustrations used to decorate or to inform. Try to discover the names and addresses of the design companies, and make a list.

The next step is to recognize which area of the market your work is suited to, which will depend on the style and subjects that appear most often in your portfolio. This is where your research can help to guide you. To assist you in contacting your market there are a number of guides that publish lists of names and addresses of design, advertising, and greetings card companies as well as book and magazine publishers.

Most companies that commission illustration are interested in seeing new artists' work, and are quite approachable either by letter or telephone. Try to find out the name of the senior art editor or designer so you can address someone personally. A letter will usually need to be followed up by a telephone call to arrange an interview, as busy designers rarely have the time to ring you. To save you time and money traveling, try to make a number of appointments on the same day, and not too far apart.

Once you have visited a possible client, create a card index or similar reference system, in which you record the name, address, and telephone number of the company and the designer you saw, the date of the interview, and any other relevant information such as the type of work they design.

Designers looking through your portfolio will often ask for samples of your work. They may take some themselves by photocopying your work during the interview, but since photocopies are not usually of very high quality, it is always preferable to provide your own samples. Although this exercise is expensive, time-consuming, tiring, and sometimes disheartening, it is the best way for new illustrators to promote their work.

STATIONERY

Becoming a successful illustrator takes more than talent and a bulging portfolio; you must also be a professional businessperson. Creating your own business stationery will not only impress your clients but can also be used as a showcase for your illustration and design skills.

There are three basic pieces of business stationery: cards, letterheads, and compliment slips, but you can include disk envelopes and invoices. The most important of all is your business card, so if your funds are limited this is the one to start with. As this is another form of self-promotion, it is worth spending a little extra for good-quality paper and printing. Try to be as creative as possible with your design, while clearly showing your name, address, telephone and fax numbers, e-mail address, and any specialization.

LETTER OF INTRODUCTION

If you feel a little unsure of approaching an art director directly by telephone, a letter of introduction and a few carefully chosen examples of your work can do the same job. However, take care over the wording of your letter; it must be one that will impress a prospective client.

Good letter
1 *The illustrator's letterhead is a good way of grabbing the Art Ed's attention.*
2 *Brief and to the point.*
3 *Follow up this letter with a phone call a few days later.*

Bad letter
1 *Find out the name of the Art Director before you write.*
2 *Proofread your letter properly before you send it out.*
3 *Enclose copies of two or three of your best pieces printed or photocopied onto one sheet.*
4 *No one's interested in seeing how your work has progressed. They are interested in seeing what you are capable of doing now.*
5 *If you want material returned you should enclose a stamped, self-addressed envelope. But why ask for material to be returned? Let the Art Director hang on to it as a reminder of who you are.*

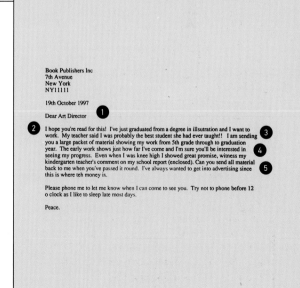

The professional portfolio

AN ILLUSTRATOR'S MOST VALUABLE POSSESSION IS PROBABLY HIS OR HER PORTFOLIO AND ITS CONTENTS, AS IT IS THE STYLE AND QUALITY OF THE WORK IN IT WHICH WILL IMPRESS FUTURE CLIENTS. IT IS VITAL THEREFORE THAT YOU SHOULD SPEND TIME DESIGNING THE LAYOUT TO INCLUDE ONLY YOUR BEST WORK.

The first decision is what style and size of portfolio to choose. There are many types and makes of portfolio on the market, from light cardboard and corrugated plastic files (which are used to store paper and sketches), to 23 × 35 in.-sized (A1) ring files with plastic sleeves and carrying handles. The industry standard portfolio is a black, 11 × 17 in. (A3) ring file with plastic pockets, and this is the recommended format if you are purchasing your first book. You may find that some of your work does not fit into this format; if it is the majority, then you will need to get a larger portfolio. Remember that the bigger it gets, the more difficult it is to display in a confined space, and as most designers tend to work in cramped conditions, wielding an ungainly book can be difficult and embarrassing.

How you design the layout of your book will obviously depend on the size and type of your work. The only golden rules are to keep the layout ordered and as simple as possible, making sure that the work is securely fixed in the sleeve, and to make sure the sleeves are clean. A useful tip is to wipe them with a rag dipped in lighter fuel, as this will remove dirt and grease, and dries very quickly.

HOW TO DESIGN YOUR PORTFOLIO: 1

The plastic sleeves in a portfolio are bought with a black sheet of sugar paper insert, and this is the usual backing for the work. Gray is also suitable as it is also a neutral color. Remember to attach your work firmly to the back sheet with a strong adhesive or double-sided tape.

Try to use only one image per side in your book, as this simplifies the design and consequently shows your work to its best advantage.

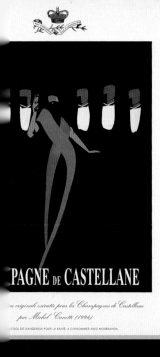

PAGNE de CASTELLANE

re originale exécutée pour les Champagnes de Castellane
par Michel Canetti (1994)

COOL EST DANGEREUX POUR LA SANTÉ. A CONSOMMER AVEC MODÉRATION.

Attach each individual image to a separate backing sheet, as you may wish to remove or rearrange the work in the future. Try to include work commissioned by your most prestigious clients, as this will help to impress future ones.

Try to keep your portfolio portrait format as in this example, as having to turn your book constantly can be distracting. If you have to mount the work landscape, place it all so it faces in the same direction.

If you have a piece of work that spans a double-page spread in a magazine, as in this example, you will find that it will not fit into a single sleeve in your portfolio. Trim the edges and mount it into two sleeves opposite each other,

LES AMBASSADEURS DE LA FÊTE

Palais russes ou Roland-Garros, dîners de gala ou privés, Potel & Chabot déploie son savoir-faire : gastronomie créative, organisation parfaite qui se fait oublier pour le seul plaisir des invités.

Comment contenter à la fois les princes qui nous gouvernent ou les créateurs de mode, contribuer au lancement d'un parfum ou d'un film, ou plus simplement rendre un goûter d'enfance inoubliable ? L'expérience, répond Potel & Chabot, la faculté d'adaptation, l'envie qui aucune soirée ne ressemble à une autre, et un certain goût du « challenge ». Comme de réunir trois cents maîtres d'hôtel professionnels, prévenants... et mesurant tous plus de 1,85 m pour répondre aux exigences de Hilton McConnico, metteur en scène de la soirée d'inauguration de la FNAC-Étoile « Nous travaillons le plus en amont possible avec les entreprises », explique Yves Le Naour. Ambassadeur de la gastronomie française, Potel & Chabot se veut également un support de communication à part entière, capable de « coller » à l'image du client. Ce n'est pas la même chose d'organiser la présentation de *Talons aiguilles*, le dernier film de Pedro Almodóvar, ou de servir trente-quatre chefs d'État dans la galerie des glaces du château de Versailles, à l'issue d'une conférence au sommet. Ce que Potel & Chabot réussit avec autant de brio. Numéro un d'une profession qu'il a largement contribué à faire évoluer, Potel & Chabot mise sans cesse sur la créativité, tant dans l'organisation des réceptions que dans les mets proposés. Sous l'impulsion de son jeune chef, Jean-Pierre Biffi, formé aux meilleurs fourneaux, Potel & Chabot s'est doté d'une véritable carte où se marient finesse, légèreté et imagination. « Du vrai, du bon et du frais », proclame Jean-Pierre Biffi, qui recherche inlassablement l'authenticité et redoute par-dessus tout la monotonie. Une prouesse lorsqu'il s'agit de servir pendant les quinze jours du tournoi de Roland-Garros pas moins de 57 000 prestations. Plus qu'un village-une ville ! Même s'il faut pour cela installer une cuisine laboratoire entièrement démontable avec ses quatre-vingt-dix cuisiniers. Ambassadeur de la gastronomie, de la fête, Potel & Chabot devait logiquement exporter son savoir-faire à l'étranger. Pressentant l'ouverture et le développement du pays de l'Est, le traiteur de la rue de Chaillot s'est implanté dès 1988 à Moscou. Avec un succès qui l'a conduit à poursuivre à Saint-Pétersbourg, en s'installant dans le palais princier Youssoupov. Fantaisie de l'Histoire lorsque l'on se souvient qu'il était autrefois le fournisseur de la cour impériale de Russie. Après Prague l'année dernière, Potel & Chabot poursuivra sa descente du Danube avec pour prochaines étapes Budapest, puis Vienne. A New York aussi, depuis 1985, Potel & Chabot apporte aux soirées de prestige la French-touch, faite d'originalité et de raffinement. Dans les palais russes comme dans ces trois splendides pavillons parisiens, pour un dîner de faste ou un brunch, Potel & Chabot a conquis son titre d'ambassadeur itinérant du bon goût.

Le haute gastronomie Potel & Chabot : légèreté, finesse et fraîcheur. Le bon goût : simplicité et authenticité. L'imagination au service de la fête.

HOW TO DESIGN YOUR PORTFOLIO: 2

An illustrator's portfolio is a showcase of his or her work, consequently each will be totally different in style and feel, as demonstrated by comparing the example on the previous page with the portfolio featured here. Most illustrators have one distinctive style. If you have more than one style, make sure that you order the book into different sections, so that the styles are separated.

In this example, the illustrator demonstrates how to design a portfolio page to show further the versatility of her illustrations, whilst also creating an extremely successful design in its own right, that would impress even the most fussy of designers.

Quite often an illustration will be reproduced in different ways, as in this example, where areas of the image have been selected by the designer to act as a header and footer to a magazine article. The complete image is then reproduced on the following page. This format shows the versatility of an illustration, when mounted in the portfolio in this way.

horoscopes

FIND OUT WHAT THE STARS HAVE IN STORE FOR YOU   THIS MONTH

Gemini
MAY 22 – JUNE 21

...y on top form during your birthday month. What is special about this year is that Mercury, Venus and Mars are all making their way towards the Sun in Gemini, and you no longer have the heavy-duty responsibilities of Saturn to contend with. You've come a long way in terms

any p... in your stride. The New Moon on the 16th adds to your general sense of joie de vivre, but it is the vibrant connection of Venus and Mars on the 23rd which sets your pulse truly racing. If you now know what you want, you are certain to get within reach of it in June.

SHE LINE MONTHLY STARS 0891 204303   WEEKLY STARS 0891 204315

Cancer JUNE 22 – JULY 23
Retreating into your shell is one way to deal with the subtle undercurrents that weave through your life in June. But now is a good time to examine your fears, doubts and emotional responses – only by doing so will you gain the insight that you need. Once the Sun enters Cancer on the 21st, and comes face to face with realistic Saturn on the 28th, you will know exactly what you must give up now in order to gain in the future.

SHE LINE MONTHLY STARS 0891 204304
WEEKLY STARS 0891 204316

Leo JULY 24 – AUG 23
June kicks off with a lively Full Moon in the romantic sphere of your chart, and this is just the enticement you need to throw off your shackles once and for all. It seems that some of your contacts and friendships are carrying rather a lot of emotional baggage. You may have to remove yourself from those people and situations that weigh you down, so it's timely that the New Moon on the 16th urges you to seek out more positive alliances.

SHE LINE MONTHLY STARS 0891 204305
WEEKLY STARS 0891 204317 ▶

CALL OUR STAR & TAROT HOTLINES

Debbie Frank's weekly and monthly horoscope hotlines provide a more detailed forecast for your star sign.

We have recently introduced Debbie's new Tarot line. Call 0891 252962 for your individual Tarot reading, which provides a unique insight into your personality and the powerful forces at work in your life.

BERTRAND
LE PAUTREMAT

Date de naissance : 19 août 1954.

Lieu de résidence : Paris.

Tranches de vie : Je viens de porter plainte pour viol, contre un quidam qui m'avait demandé l'heure.

Points forts : Organisation interne du pliage et travail sur la lumière pour enrichir les transparences.

Influences : Henri Michaux a écrit : "L'homme naît avec vingt-deux plis. Il s'agit de les déplier. La vie de l'homme, alors, est complète."

Illustrateurs préférés : Calder, Beuys, Fontana, Kollar, Christo, Lissitsky et Archipenko pour le constructivisme.

Le meilleur prix pour un boulot : Le pont d'or.

Le travail le plus passionnant : Plier, pour libérer le sujet aperçu dans la feuille.

Le travail le plus déprimant : Le vide dans la feuille.

Amours : Les Touaregs pour leur économie de moyens et leur sens de l'essentiel. Le plaisir qu'il y a à toucher du papier du bout des doigts.

Haines : Tout ce qui altère la conscience, et tous les ghettos.

A emporter pour quelques jours de solitude : "Les préceptes de l'indifférence" du Dalaï Lama, du papier et surtout une crème anti-rides.

Téléphone : 42 27 54 00.

Agent : Allain François.

6

7

ILLUSTRATEUR DU MOIS

On this portfolio page the illustrator displays prints of her original artwork and shows how a similar piece works in the context of the printed page. This provides variety for anyone flipping through the folio and shows how the idea has been sustained over several star signs.

THE UNACCOMPANIED PORTFOLIO

Many companies, particularly advertising agencies, will only see a portfolio unaccompanied by its illustrator. In these cases it is a good idea to have a short resumé of your work and a full client list to introduce your book for you. Include a photograph of yourself, as this will help the designer put a name to a face.

THEMES

Looking at the work of other professionals is interesting and instructive for both the full-time illustrator and the beginner. It is always exciting to see the many different styles and ways of using the wide range of techniques and mediums available to illustrators. For beginners, learning by example not only provides technical ideas but will also help them decide on their own individual style, while a professional may be inspired to create a new style or perfect an existing one. The gallery that follows is intended to provide this inspiration, whatever your chosen field of illustration. It is divided into sections grouped according to subject matter, such as food and drink, humans and animals, conceptual illustration, and children's and technical illustration. The images have been chosen from a cross-section of the work of some of the most successful and creative illustrators from all around the world. They show a wide range of styles, techniques and mediums, analysed in detail to give you an understanding of the creative processes and individual method of the artists.

LEFT *Charles Thompson*
For this exquisitely detailed illustration, the artist has used a traditional painting medium, oil paint on canvas. Oil paint is not a medium often favored for illustration work, as it takes a long time to dry, which is a problem if you are working to a tight deadline. But if you like the effects of oils, you can imitate them with the newly developed alkyds, which have similar properties but a much faster drying time.

RIGHT *Adam Willis*
The airbrush is one of the most flexible illustration tools. In the hands of a skilled and creative artist it can create a wide variety of effects from photo-realism to images that mimic other techniques, as in this example. By careful shading and the use of a monochrome palette, the illustrator has created an image that gives the impression of a low-relief sculpture. He has used a splattercap nozzle to apply a random pours texture, which was then overworked with flat layers of pigment to describe the shadows.

Children's illustration

This field is one that allows the illustrator considerable scope for creativity and imagination, and many illustrators are attracted to it for this reason. As can be seen from the examples shown on these pages, it is open to any medium but is better suited to a representational rather than an abstract or highly stylized approach.

LEFT
Maki Kashiwabara
A factor in the increasing popularity of paper sculpture as an illustration technique is that in recent years paper manufacturers have produced new ranges of colored and textured papers. For this example the artist has been able to choose a whole palette of ready made pastel colors which are wholly appropriate for this particular market.

ABOVE
Eiichi Isokawa
Acrylic paints can be blended in a number of ways, and here the illustrator has used a technique similar to that employed by oil painters, laying down strips of color that are merged by stroking and wiping with the brush. Because acrylic dries quickly, this method is facilitated by adding acrylic retarder to the paint on the palette.

Ainslie Macleod

Pen and wash drawing is a traditional medium for both humorists and children's illustrators, and in this illustration the style has been imitated by the computer. The usual method is to start with a freehand sketch which is then scanned into the computer and manipulated on-screen. This allows the artist to exploit both the expressive qualities of a freehand drawing and the full range of creative possibilities offered by the computer.

ABOVE
Hitomi Fuse
This powerful image of St. Michael shows that watercolor need not be a wishy-washy medium. The artist has built up the paint in layers, using a palette of yellow ocher, raw umber, and sepia to create a color scheme reminiscent of old parchment.

RIGHT
Alison Forsythe
Gouache, if used in its concentrated form straight out of the tube, is a fully opaque medium, which makes it ideal for painting large areas of completely flat color. The design of this illustration is reminiscent of modern South American popular art, which makes use of the same intense, saturated flat colors in conjunction with a stylized, slightly naive technique.

Glenn Wright

Oil paints are not a medium often favored by illustrators because they take a long time to dry, which creates difficulties if you are working on a short deadline. But modern technology has now produced a range of alkyd paints which give the same effects as oils but dry in half the time, and it is these that have been used for this illustration. The artist has worked in a broad, oil-painterly style, using the surface of the canvas to add extra texture to the image.

ABOVE
Guy Passey

In this example, colored pencil has been used in a series of careful layers to build up the depth of pigment, producing intense, fully saturated color. The artist has used dry colored pencil throughout, and this has enabled him to create texture in the sky above the horizon. If you look closely you can see how he has applied the color in a series of fine lines suggesting the rays of the setting sun.

Jean Hirashima

Creating a strong composition is important in any illustration, illustration, but in the field of humor it becomes a vital part of the story-telling process, directing the eye around the image. In this example the artist has used a strong diagonal, so that attention is drawn first to the major element—the boat—and then upward along the fishing rod to the dog, the scissors, and finally the baby hanging over the hungry crocodiles. This compositional device has enabled the artist to reveal the joke gradually, saving the "punch line" for the end.

Viv Eisner-Hess

Animals are a common theme in children's illustration, and finding quick and successful techniques for rendering fur and feathers makes the busy illustrator's job much easier. In "Animal Ark," one of twelve paintings for a calendar, in gouache and colored pencil, the artist has built up textures by color overlays and dry-brushing. For the birds, she has used a method not dissimilar to embroidery, where long and short stitches are used to stagger interchanging colors. In painting this is done with long and short strokes of paint, with the next color added with a long stroke following on from the short one of the other color.

LEFT
Pol Turgeon
The concept for this piece could possibly be vacation reading matter, with the little palm tree, the midday sun, the ice-cream cone, and the wheels and handles of the cart implying the book's mobility. This artist has used acrylic pigments that have been deliberately "aged" with crackle varnish.

RIGHT
John S. Dykes
Banks and computer companies are a strong market for concept art. The client for this illustration was the Harvard Business School, the concept "the ethics maze." The image is simple but eloquent; the way the maze disappears into the blue distance and bleeds off the edge of the picture gives the impression that it stretches on to infinity.

Conceptua
illustration

Illustration is an extremely po|

communication. One of its

compared to, for instance, photog|

the possibility of interpreting abs|

through a single image. As can |

shown in this section, conceptua|

artist the opportunity to create ne|

as it is less bound by normal |

forms, and demands a very differ|

Sarah Kelly
Collage is an especially suitable medium for conceptual illustration, as it allows the artist to juxtapose numerous images on the page, representing the different concepts and ideas often demanded by the subject. In this image of a dreaming girl, the artist has used found objects and materials alongside images cut from magazines, the composition being held together by a painted frame of the night sky.

Hitomi Ueki
Collage meets model making in this three-dimensional illustration for the cover of a brochure. The materials include twisted wire, the cogs from a small clock, screw-heads, a variety of little beads, cut metal and the wheels from a toy car. The body of the truck is made from colored modeling clay.

Melanie Barnes
This mixed-media and collage illustration was commissioned for a book jacket. The artist has collected some wonderful items to work into the collage, including shells, shoes from an Edwardian pattern book, antique clock face papers, old gramophone needles, an Indian stamp and a little toy soldier.

Jane Whitaker

The title of this illustration, used as a T-shirt design, is "Natural Balance," and the idea is expressed by the figure's juggling action. The artist has employed lithography and woodcut techniques, in a style reminiscent of African sculpture, which was the inspiration for the piece. The technique, style, and muted color scheme convey the idea of something natural, which is inherent to the theme.

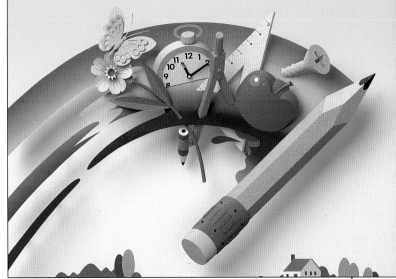

LEFT
Sophie Marsham

For the figures, the artist has collaged a variety of hard materials, mostly metal and glass. Each has its own individual character, and is made from different found objects. A pair of antique clippers forms the body of the one on the left; his eyes are washers, and one arm is a spanner.

Hideharu Naitoh

Paper sculpture is becoming an increasingly popular technique for illustrators because it offers the opportunity to give a three-dimensional quality to flat artwork. The background of this image was made from cut paper, and the rainbow and small objects were then created by carefully cutting and scoring textured colored papers, which are set at different distances from the background. The whole design was then carefully lit before being photographed.

Environment

These four pages show illustrations of landscape and architecture, both useful subjects to include in your portfolio. As can be seen here and throughout the "Themes" section of the book, each image differs even when the subjects are similar. This is due partly to the choice of technique and medium, but more importantly, to each illustrator's unique and individual style.

RIGHT
Maggie Ling
This wonderfully humorous illustration, "Deadline," expresses more about the nightmare of moving house than any amount of words. The medium is ink and wash, favored by many humorous artists because it enables an image to be created quickly. It is also highly expressive, the dip pen giving a wonderful variety of line qualities, and the wash then adding color and solidity of form.

Ann Tout
In the past, before the days of color printing, the technique used for most book illustration was wood engraving, and here the artist has drawn on the same tradition, but has used linoleumcut to give her work a more modern feel. Linoleum-cut is a much broader and thus more expressive medium, as demonstrated by the lively and dynamic effects in the sky and foreground.

BELOW
Nicola Gregory
Architectural illustration need
not be merely technical; the
approach will depend on the
purpose of the commission.
For this hotel brochure, the
artist has used a very loose
watercolor technique to create
a lively, impressionistic image
whose appeal is enhanced by
the choice of vivid colors.

Jane Dodds

Typography and decorative lettering can form an exciting element in an image, and skill in this field can open up new illustration markets. In this design the artist demonstrates her understanding of letter forms and their decorative possibilities. Each sign on the shop front uses one or two different type faces, giving each one its own individuality. Other markets for decorative type include maps and book jacket titles.

LEFT
Peter Byatt

The travel industry is an extensive market for illustrators, and is the one the artist is targeting in this self-promotional illustration. As in the brochure (far left), he has used watercolors in a broad wash style, but here the marks of the brush play a strong role in the composition. Notice especially the varied and expressive marks in the sky and in the foreground water.

Caroline Thomson

Alkyd paints have an advantage over oil paints for the illustrator in that they dry much more rapidly. This does make it more difficult to blend colors, but there are a number of ways of doing this. In this illustration the artist has created a soft, almost mossy effect by a method known as optical blending, which involves laying on small dots of color which appear to mix when seen at a distance, much like the dots in a printed image. This effect is most obvious in the shadows on the topiary and in the transition of colors in the sky.

Food and drink

Food and drink are both major industries, so it is not surprising that their products are among the most commonly commissioned illustration subjects, appearing in magazines, on book jackets and on supermarket packaging. As subjects for the illustrator they are ideal, as they allow a wide range of interpretation from highly detailed work to extremely loose and expressive images, and can be rendered in any of the techniques available to the illustrator.

Mark McLaughlin
This is a style much favored by magazine designers, ideal for a decorative illustration to be used alongside a body of text. It uses watercolor in a controlled but loose technique, with a series of broad washes gradually worked into when dry to add more definition.

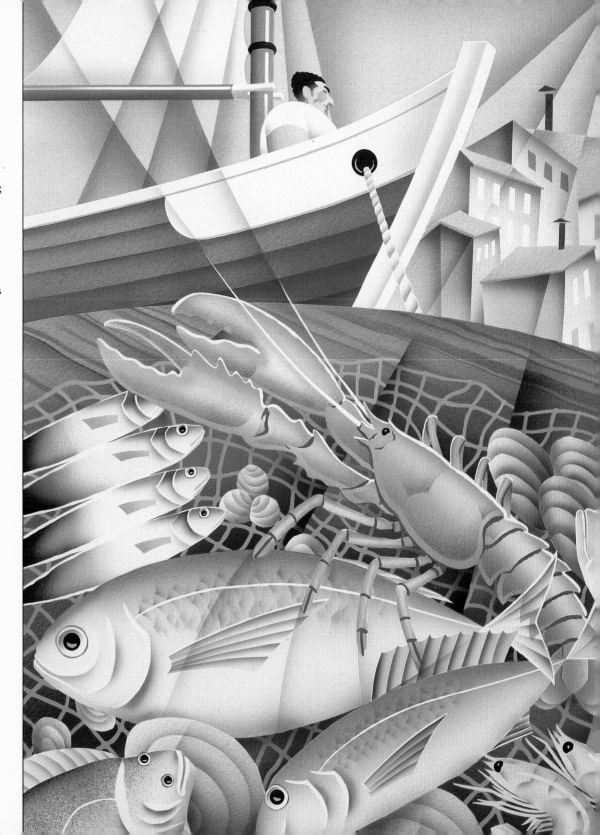

Terry Hand

In both fine art and illustration there is a long tradition of artists paying homage to earlier masters by adapting styles of the past to their own work. In this airbrush illustration promoting a fish restaurant, the artist has used the ideas of Cubism, developed by Picasso and Braque, to create a dynamic composition. Masking techniques have been used to dissect the image along a series of lines emanating from the top right-hand corner.

LEFT
Graham Berry

In this image the illustrator has combined two very different watercolor techniques. In the foreground there is a high degree of worked wet-on-dry, while the background is loosely painted, wet-in-wet. This contrast, together with the use of strong shadows and dark tones in the background, brings the white china forward in space and gives it strength and solidity.

Gilles Cenazandotti
This type of three-dimensional
illustration, where model-
making and collage overlap, is
becoming increasingly popular
in illustration. In this example,
made for a supermarket, the
illustrator has used colored
corrugated cardboard cut,
folded, and painted, to create a
delightfully appetizing image.

ABOVE
Patrick Jones
One of the most notable
features of the airbrush is its
ability to produce photo-realist
images by building up layers
of pigment. In this case the
artist has also used a scraping
technique, making the
highlights on the beans, plate,
tomato, toast, and so on, by
carefully removing pigment
with a scalpel to leave the
white board visible. This
technique is most successful on
a very smooth Hot-Press
illustration board.

Catharine Slade
In this little flight of fancy, quite saturated watercolor washes were used to produce intense colors in the center of the image. The small stars were painted over the blue with white gouache. The decorative border was made with graduated washes, and detail added using a dry-brush technique.

ABOVE
Catharine Slade
For this magazine illustration the artist used watercolors made from man-made pigment. These, which are widely available, are especially suitable for mass printing processes; the more subtle vegetable pigments can sometimes print badly. Attention was also paid to heightening the contrast between light and shade .

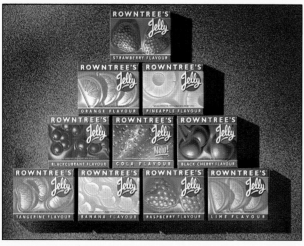

ABOVE AND LEFT
Adam Willis
Packaging illustration, especially for food, demands extremely colorful and eye-catching work, as seen in these two airbrushed illustrations for Rowntree's jelly, in which the artist has used the high shine and color of the fruit to produce a background for the typography. It is important to remember that an illustration has to do a job: to convey information, to be decorative, or both. Unless you remember this, you may be shocked to find how little of your illustration is visible once printed, with the typography in place.

Dan Crisp
Layers of opaque gouache were used to create this photo-realist strawberry, painted considerably larger than life-size. By minute changes of tone between the background color and the slightly darker shadow, the artist has given the impression of modeling around each seed. To heighten the effect, tiny areas of white gouache were painted around the depression and a larger area added as a highlight.

Samuel Salfino
Border designs, which make a decorative frame for a body of text, are another quite common commission. These are used both in magazine advertising and in food packaging. A graded yellow background has been added to give a background to half of this airbrushed illustration.

Human and animal

Most illustrators will be called upon to exercise their skills in at least one of these two fields, and a competent grasp of anatomy is required for this kind of subject. A strong grounding in traditional techniques is also a good springboard from which to experiment and find your own style.

Kan Daba
This illustration eloquently demonstrates the reason for the increasing popularity of computer-generated illustration, which enables the artist to create images that seem almost true to life. In this little fantasy a complete world has been created, with a convincing impression of depth and three-dimensional form as well as a range of different textures, from the softness of Santa's beard to the metallic sheen on the fairy.

Hirofumi Maruko
Another sample of the extraordinary effects possible with computer-generated illustration. The impression of highly polished metal is enhanced by the separate reflection on each panel of the birds. If you look closely at the head of the foreground bird you can see mirrored on its surface a reflection of the clouds above it.

Mitsuru Todoriki
Anthropomorphism – giving human attributes to animals – has a long tradition in illustration, evidenced by the work of E. H. Shephard and Arthur Rackham among others. In this airbrush illustration, in which woodland animals sing karaoke style, the artist has continued the tradition.

Adam Willis
A style slightly reminiscent of Russian poster art has been used for this airbrush illustration, a promotional piece for Nestlé. To give additional drama to the scene, the artist has used a limited palette of colors. The background is divided into two by these same two colors, with the clothes of the figures mirroring them in the foreground.

Mamoru Matsusato
This is an excellent example of the inventive use of acrylic impasto to create pattern and texture. The swirling texture of the background was applied first, with impasto medium, and color was laid on top when this had dried. Portions of the board have been left flat, to give fuller definition to the figures and faces.

Tetsu Tomida
For this traditional representation of a young girl, the artist has chosen the medium of pastel, which has enabled him to give a soft, glowing quality to the picture, reminiscent of the paintings of Renoir. To ensure that the eye is drawn to the face of the young girl, the artist has concentrated the most detail in this area; the rest of the body and dress are less worked, and the background is only lightly suggested.

Cerys Edwards
Creating an individual style by which an illustrator becomes identified can often open up new career prospects. A style can be molded by a technique, or by the way objects and images are interpreted, as in this image. Although we can identify the animal as a cat, it is heavily stylized, as are all the other objects in the design.

Viv Eisner-Hess
Opaque pigments—a mix of
acrylic and gouache—were
used in this illustration,
enabling the artist to build up
vibrant, intense color and to
superimpose fine detail. The
illustration was commissioned
as one of twelve for a
calendar, and the individual
images were also reproduced
as greetings cards.

Takahiro Kanie
This wonderfully vivid
illustration demonstrates the
possibilities of acrylic for
creating powerful contrasts of
tone and color. The depth and
intensity of the blue in the sea
contrasts with the light tones
and startlingly vivid colors of
the little reef fish, which stand
out in strong relief.

Technical illustration

Technical illustration is a wide field, embracing subjects as diverse as natural history, medical, mechanical, architectural, and scientific illustration. This form of illustration demands not only the ability to draw accurately and understand painting techniques, but also an in-depth knowledge of a specialist subject. And because most technical illustration involves a high level of detail, it also needs a good deal of patience.

Hide Nakajima
In this image, a tour-de-force of the technical illustrator's art, commissioned by Mitsubishi, the airbrush is used in what is perhaps its most traditional manner, in conjunction with masking film. The areas of the image are repeatedly masked and then sprayed, enabling the artist to produce a highly detailed cut-away.

RIGHT
Adam Willis
Technical illustration need not be humorless, as this illustration shows. Because of the high finish and degree of detail and realism that can be achieved with the airbrush, it is possible to create an imaginary world that almost seems to be real.

LEFT
Dave Higginson
As an image commissioned for a direct mail envelope this would have caught many people's eye as it dropped through their mail box. The painstaking copy of a small area of a British banknote, created from a web of decorative motifs described by fine parallel lines, reminds us that the art of the illustrator is evident even in the money in our pockets.

Julian Aspinall
The airbrush is perhaps the most popular medium for rendering highly reflective surfaces such as glass and metal. But producing an illustration like this is not just a matter of technical skill; it also requires a solid knowledge of light and shade and the way they model forms to make objects appear solid and three-dimensional.

RIGHT
Charles Thompson
The airbrush is not the only medium that is able to create photo-realist effects; oil paint was the medium chosen for this dramatic image. The artist has exploited the creamy consistency of the paint, which allows colors to be smeared and moved around on the canvas, to imitate the texture of soft, windblown snow. The realistic effect is enhanced by strong use of light and shade.

BELOW
Catherine Diez-Luckie
In this self-promotion piece the artist has successfully demonstrated her skill at rendering glass, working with an airbrush and acrylic paint on illustration board. She has used lighting that provides strong light-dark contrasts, which have helped her to produce the effect of three-dimensional forms. The objects themselves are almost in twilight, but with clearly shaped highlights.

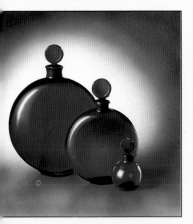

Tetsuya Mizuno
The main task of a technical illustration is to provide a visual aid showing how things are constructed or how they will look, or might look, once completed. In this example, "Try 2004," a futuristic building takes on reality through skillful use of the airbrush and knowledge of building techniques.

Anita S. Bice
A good technical illustration says more than a thousand words. In this airbrushed example the artist has produced a straightforward visual description, demonstrating in simple graphic terms the construction of a proposed new factory. A technical illustrator must have an interest in structure and function as well as an understanding of basic geometry and mechanical perspective.

Anita S. Bice
The style should suit the subject. For this classical architectural pediment the artist has used a much softer style than in her illustration of the factory (left), working within the tradition of architect's drawings.

Michael Courtney
Medical illustration, as with the other forms of technical illustration, depends on a thorough understanding of the subject.

Index

Credits

Quarto would like to thank all the artists who have kindly allowed us to reproduce their work in this book.

We are indebted to the following artists' agents for their interest in and generous contribution to this project: Jon Hughes at LONDON ART COLLECTION, 24 Goodge Street, London W1, representing Julian Aspinall, Graham Berry, Michel Canetti, Dan Crisp, Lee Crocker, Jane Dodds, Cerys Edwards, Alison Forsythe, Nicola Gregory, Dave Higginson, Patrick Jones, Sarah Kelly, Ainslie Macleod, Bertrand le Pautremat, Charles Thompson, Adam Willis, and Glenn Wright; Takahiro Kanie at CREARE, 806 Daiyahaitsu Nakanosakaue, 2-48-9 Honcho Nakano-Ku, Tokyo, Japan, representing Hitomi Fuse, Eiichi Isokawa, Takahiro Kanie, Maki Kashiwabara, Hirofumi Maruko, Mamoru Matsusato, Tetsuya Mizuno, Hideharu Naitoh, Hide Nakajima, Nagako Suzuki, Mitsuru Todoriki, and Tetsu Tomida; Sylvie Witkam at ARTBOX BV, Kruilaan 182, 1098 SK Amsterdam, Netherlands, representing Paola Piglia and Pol Turgeon; Mariko Akimaru at SUGAR INC, Akasaka-Mori bldg, 8-13-23 Akasaka, Minato-Ku, Japan, Tokyo, representing Kan Daba and Hitomi Ueki; and Valérie Schermann at PRIMA LINEA, 143 rue d'Alesia, 75014 Paris, France, representing Gilles Cenazandotti.

All other artists may be contacted through Quarto.

Additional credits: portfolio pages appear on pages 120, 132–3 (Michel Canetti) and page 135 (Bertrand le Pautremat) by courtesy of London Art Collection. Peter Bartczak trades as Clownbank Studio; Anita S. Bice as Commercial Artistry; Peter Gudynas is a founder of Zap Art. Sophie Marsham's sculptures (pages 28 and 148) were photographed by Martin Griffin.

Quarto would like to thank all the artists who contributed to the demonstrations – Julie Anderson, Sian Burston, Janie Coath, Joanna Cameron, Gary Cross, Nina Davies, Jane Dennis, Russell Harvey, Dave Kemp, Ian Sidaway, Catharine Slade, Anne Tout.

Every effort has been made to credit all copyright holders. Quarto would like to apologise should any omissions have been made.